TAO Management

TAO Management

Japanese Management Philosophy
Based on an Interpretation
of the *Tao Te Ching*

Yoshifumi Taguchi

EastBridge

Copyright © 2006 by Yoshifumi Taguchi

EastBridge is a nonprofit publishing corporation, chartered in the State of Connecticut and tax exempt under section 501(c)(3) of the United States tax code.

Library of Congress Cataloging-in-Publication Data

[Cataloging-in-Publication data for this book has been applied for from the Library of Congress]

Printed in the United States of America

Contents

Preface

THIS BOOK DEALS WITH JAPANESE MANAGEMENT PHILOSOPHY, based upon an interpretation of Chinese philosophy, *Lao-zi* (*Lao-tzu* or *Tao Te Ching*). Since the bursting of the bubble economy in Japan during the early 1990s, prominent business executives in Japan have been engaged in much soul-searching. During the Meiji Restoration just after the opening of Japan in the 1850s and in the post-World War II period, Japanese top executives endeavored to build a modern Japan while learning the principles of Chinese Confucian philosophy through the interpretation of *The Analects of Confucius*. Recently, many economists have come to understand Japan's industrial revitalization, which has resulted from the strenuous restructuring efforts of Japan's top executives. One could attribute Japan's industrial resuscitation to the introduction of a Western-style management approach. However, many Japanese business leaders regard their intellectual backbone to be the principles expressed in ancient Chinese philosophy, including *Lao-zi* (*Lao-tzu* or *Tao Te Ching*), *Taxue* (*Great Learning*), as well as *The*

中国思想
老子

儒教
論語

古典中国思想
大学
大学

Analects. This book tries to provide the reader with an understanding of *Lao-zi* in order to make clear the attitudes of business leaders in Japan.

This work has benefited from the encouragement and deft English translation of Dr. Susan J. Newton. My colleagues at my company, Image Plan, helped with necessary information and references. My friend Jun Kurihara, a senior fellow at the John F. Kennedy School of Harvard University, wished me well and found the good U.S. company, EastBridge, to publish this book in English. To all these people, I express my heartfelt appreciation for their contributions.

Yoshifumi Taguchi, President, Image Plan

Introduction

Tao — the Origin

THE COSMOS THAT WE INHABIT originated with the Tao. Other traditions refer to it as Lord of the universe, God, or the Creator. In the beginning, the Tao opened up the universe that in turn, gave birth to all existence — from animals, plants, and trees to mountains, seas, and the human race. Therefore, nothing in the world exists that has not been touched by the Tao. Thus, everything may be considered an "alter ego" of the Tao.

This "second-self" is one part of the Tao, and as humans are a natural element of this second-self, we directly inherit the Tao nature. Unfortunately, we tend to completely forget about this heritage and often become separated from the essence of the Tao. It is precisely this essence that is supreme in the natural world and across its populations. Therefore, it would be highly beneficial for us to turn our attention to study the Tao, and endeavor to remember our direct link to this essence. The posture that the Tao adopts in its relations to all things is the finest model available, and to lead our lives in accordance with the Tao is to conduct ourselves in the best way possible as humans.

The corporate world is no exception: the company and all its organizational elements exist because of the influence of the Tao. Succinctly, we can say that all corporate activity and business is the Tao in action. Thus, it is clearly appropriate for us to study the essence of the Tao as a way to excellence in the company and corporate world as well.

The Tao in Practice

Working in alignment with the Tao reduces the frequency and severity of any delay, stoppage, or failure, and so lessens the possibility of things going contrary to what we hope to achieve. Can there be any kind of work in corporate management that would not benefit from the assistance of such energy? When merchandise is being developed, ideas, designs, and technological breakthroughs would all clearly profit from such support. In the production phase, the delicate timing of combining different materials and the shaping of complicated forms are all its results, and in sales, that which causes a product to become a best-seller is also the energy of the cosmos in action.

Conflicts or disputes with things are rare while working with the Tao, so work proceeds to flow along harmoniously. When there is an absence of hostility and contention, a cooperative spirit is awakened and leads to a pooling of strengths, in turn resulting in a peaceful workplace with a high frequency of pleasant and rewarding human relations.

Regarding customer relations, because dispute is rare between the supplier and user, the company naturally makes products that will truly satisfy the customer while the customer cooperates to ensure that he or she obtains a perfect product as well as one that is really desired. In other words, both sides engage in the manufacture of the product with mutual effort, resulting in a "made to order" situation.

Through the process of making such a satisfactory product, the customer comes to be in alignment with the company's policy, rather than merely a purchaser of the product. The pleased and sympathetic customer will inevitably want to convey the merits of the product to those around him or her (in effect recommending that product) and so, the satisfied customer will become a salesperson. This ever-widening circle of support will eventually reach worldwide and naturally confer global status on the company. Although there are many companies in the world, the enterprise that frees itself from competition will become the only one that manufactures a particular product; it therefore becomes an "Only One enterprise" and will channel the cost of competition into reinforcing its uniqueness. Thus, a non-competitive market is created and fostered.

Management that embraces the Tao will become the most natural kind of management, progressing smoothly and ensuring that business proceeds as planned. In other words, "Ideal Management" will be made possible.

Jozen wa mizu gotoshi. The most natural kind of management that follows the Tao comes to function in harmony with the smooth fluidity of water. Like water, it skillfully permeates into empty spaces creating a vital and refreshing, all-cleansing dynamism.

The Tao as Mother — Partnership in Harmony

As the Tao is the creator of all nature, so all things in this world are children of the same mother — children of the Tao. Therefore, all things are inter-related.

Our view of corporate activity must be re-adjusted to reflect this realization of the inter-relatedness of all things. For example, if we look at materials needed in the manufacture of goods in the same way as we perceive our human colleagues, then it means listening to the voices of the materials themselves, and to what they have to say to us. From this, the ideal way of making the most of the materials will become clear. The latent possibilities of the materials' elements and constituents will manifest, encouraging a very natural way of utilizing the specific, even unique qualities inherent in the materials. As a result, not only will optimum use be made of the materials' characteristics, but the production stage of bending, stretching, and putting materials together will proceed effortlessly while both losses and superfluous power usage are minimized. If competitors are seen as our interrelated colleagues, the resulting cooperative attitude will enable the customers' needs to be optimally addressed in the most natural way, and the expanding market will enable all sides to benefit profitably. In this way, the changes in corporate management caused by the shift from an underlying concept of rivalry to one of harmonious partnership will naturally lead to expansion of the company's potential in and of itself, as well as bringing us closer to the best kind of corporate society.

"Management with the Tao as its ideal" and "Harmonious partnership management" do not draw conflict or encourage competition with anything. The energy presently expended on competition, from the direct cost of competing through advertising and in product promotion up through the mental burden upon those responsible for analyzing market fluctuation, will be rendered unnecessary, and the company's energy will neither be diluted nor wasted. Because the amount of energy will be maintained at a more constant level, fatigue will be far less prevalent in the company acting in this manner. A continuing contribution will be made to the advancement of society and our lives as such new values are progressively created and implemented.

Work is conducted in such a company by aligning with and smoothly incorporating the energy of the cosmos. The people involved are alert, aware, and motivated when carrying out their jobs. Consequently, there is little loss, the level of creativity is high, and the impossible becomes possible, providing society with an attractive business and its products.

Due to high levels of creativity, new business and products readily emerge so management does not have to rely solely on the "one-hit wonder" product or upon past business success. When competing enterprises release rival products or enter the same kind of market, it is already a situation where the company has opened up new ground, and is in the process of moving there. Thus, competition simply does not exist for this kind of company. We could also call this "Creative, flexible, thinking management."

Further, an enthusiasm will be created to address and deal with everything in its initial stages, and the company will readily carry out its research by keeping abreast of popular trends. This in turn will enable it to adopt appropriate strategies in applying suitable countermeasures where needed as well as consistently keeping it one step ahead of other companies when responding to people's needs.

On the other hand, negative aspects such as trouble or failure developing either inside or outside the company can be detected early and nipped in the bud before a serious situation is reached. Instead of seeking to enhance its reputation and fame in the world at large, the direction of making a true contribution to society is chosen. This results in a company that, while modest, is an active and responsive company of substance and genuine ability.

In everything, 70 percent of satisfaction is enough. The aim of company growth should be to satisfy each customer so that profits can still be maintained without striving for business expansion merely to increase size. Additional energy can be more usefully directed towards enriching the customer's satisfaction that, in turn, will lead to securing continuous orders. Such an approach nurtures the conducting of business that can develop comfortably and has room to maneuver.

No. 1 TAI-DOH 導同

Transcending Logical Reasoning

IS IT REALLY LOGICAL REASONING that conferred wisdom on mankind? In humanity's long history there 人類の歴史 has never been a prior period where logical understanding has been stressed to the extent that it is today.

Humans cannot realize a deeper ultimate truth than that which comes from direct experience. We must attend to this fully. Truth is where something can be said to be A, while, at the same time, it can also be said to be B. That is, as soon as we have expressed something in words, we become separated from its essential nature and end up straying from the truth. For example, how could we accurately describe a horse to someone who has never seen one? We could say: "a tame animal" or "a ferocious beast"; "a docile animal" or "a fastidious animal"; "a huge animal (compared to a dog)" or "a medium-sized animal (compared to an elephant)." Therefore, actually seeing and touching, feeling and firsthand experience are mandated.

In business, the key to success is how to free oneself from the brandishing of theoretical arguments and criticism as though more than mere words. Learning through experience by application, execution, and performance needs to be adopted as the basic standard of the company; whether or not you "speak after doing" and "conclude as a result of experiencing" are of vital importance. Mastery through practical experience thus rightfully becomes the basis for the company's business and evaluation criteria.

"A corporate climate of practical experience" means that the level of knowledge attained will become the company's basic standard. Thus, more detailed and subtle problems will steadily be investigated and such research will bring about a natural accumulation of matchless expertise within the company. Further, irresponsible, empty utterances and attitudes will be rejected while a sound and reliable business attitude in the company will be fostered.

Names did not exist before the creation of the world. When the earth was created, things could not very well be called A or B, so names like "Heaven" and "Earth" were used. In other words, a name is an expedient, a mere symbol used to distinguish one thing from another. Therefore, attaching importance to names, or trying to understand people and things by basing our judgment on names, is completely meaningless.

In business, too, it is foolish to base our standard of judging and gauging respect for people upon titles. Before giving consideration to titles, we need to begin by understanding people, things, and the relationships between.

By going beyond words and names, how deeply we understand people and things through experience is of the utmost importance. If this attitude is continuously held as a matter of one's principles, the power to gain insight into a person's or thing's true quality will be obtained; thus, areas of subtlety and vagueness will become clear. Once the subtle and the vague clarify, such things as mistakes, problems, and warning signs will readily become comprehensible. The person who is able to do this is called a "professional," someone who can perceive and deal with the subtle, the vague, and the "not easily seen."

Why is it that we receive an education? The answer is, to gain the ability to learn from one's mistakes. Likewise in business, this one point forms the basic standard of "vete- ranship": the veteran repeats few mistakes whereas the new- comer makes many. As the veteran becomes even more skilled, he or she will come to be correct in matters that can- not be seen clearly. In other words, he or she will be able to anticipate and deal with the unexpected by thinking, "To- morrow, this kind of thing will probably happen, so I'd better do something about it today to prevent problems oc- curring." These, then, are the kinds of actions that serve to illuminate the obscure and to clarify otherwise subtle and vague hunches.

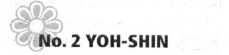

No. 2 YOH-SHIN

No Competition, No Conflict

WHEN WE EVALUATE THINGS IN THIS WORLD, such evaluation is often relative. This is also true in the business field. When we say "a large enterprise," what happens when we try to compare it to an even larger one? When we say "a good company," what can we say when an even better one appears? This kind of relative appraisal lacks accuracy as not only is the true nature of something not properly conveyed, but needless stress is also exerted on our minds. In the company, evaluating relatively by saying Mr. A is better than Mr. B creates competition that may become a negative source of ambition, although not all ambition is caused in this way. Ambition is also something more volitional and may occur because of a liking for the task at hand. We would be wise to support such positive ambition arising from the pleasure of engaging in what is felt to be enjoyable and meaningful work.

Human beings possess individuality. This is something that is characteristic of a particular person and therefore is of no use to others whatsoever. How can we talk about a human's work without recognizing the importance of individuality? Can we say that respect comes only from comparison with others? It is necessary for the company and for those who work there to increasingly distance themselves from "relative evaluation." The greater the separation, the freer we will become, and as a return is made to one's original self, individuality will be brought out while the ability that we alone have is expressed through work that we alone are capable of. This, indeed, is true human nature at work.

Until now, there has been a marked tendency for corporate organizations to value similarity. This has meant recognizing the value of how to accomplish identical work at a faster pace than others and in greater volume. It epitomizes and reflects the sense of values of the mass production and mass-selling era.

Today, emphasis is placed on how to create products that cannot be produced by other makers, which has meant a switch of emphasis from uniformity to individuality. An organization has now come to mean a group with a variety of personalities. It is this collision of the various kinds of personalities that produces wonderfully unexpected results. Here, comparing members to each other is without meaning and, because of the great personality differences, even impossible. The era of running an organization through relative evaluation has ended.

Consider the real personality of nature. The natural landscape — that scenery and those elements of nature that exist only there — asserts it own personality and it is absolute. By contrast, then, it may be clearly understood that relative evaluation is artificial. Something that is artificial is also limited and cannot last. Of highest priority now is how to eliminate such artificial elements and thinking, and to proceed in accordance with nature. The energy of nature is inexhaustible, and to work in alignment with nature means accessing the power of natural energy for development and progress on both individual as well as corporate levels. Working with this kind of spirit ensures that implementation will proceed smoothly as one feels joy in the act of actually carrying out something, or becoming "one with nature." The joy in doing our work will be experienced through meeting the many challenges encountered in bringing success to the task at hand. When successfully completed, rather than stopping and claiming possession of the results, it will become natural to seek the enjoyment and pleasure to be gained from proceeding with the challenge of fresh tasks. If one adopts this sort of consciousness, which engenders little delay or stoppage, more efficient use of natural energy and its proper application can be made, thus deepening our feeling of being at one with nature. When the others around us observe this kind of process at work on an individual level, and because the energy of nature is also active in work on the corporate level, everything will be seen as having attained excellence and be moving toward the achievement of perfection. In this way, we can earn people's confidence and respect. It is exactly the same in business.

In the realm of corporate management, the casting away of relativity and adopting of the absolute results in a "unique corporation" as it is provides the company with guiding values that do not customarily exist in the corporate world. Even on a global scale, the company that is the specialist in a given field, the sole maker and seller of a particular product, is a company that knows no such thing as competition. Thus, the factor of "competition cost," i.e., the outlay spent in competing with rival companies in advertising, sales promotion, etc., will become unnecessary. Further, if throughout the world the only way of purchasing the product is by ordering from the company, orders will come from the searches that customers do themselves, thus diminishing the need for sales and marketing. It will be a case of, "Please let me buy it." Selling costs will be minimized, and without the element of competition, no particular price

6

特別は個人名様作

manipulations will be necessary. The funds thus freed can be wholly devoted to research. Exemplifying its alignment with the principles of the natural world at work in this way, the company will thus also more fully manifest itself as a "unique enterprise."

No. 3 AN-MIN

Truth Will Again Play
the Leading Role

A SOUND, STABLE SOCIETY, OR CORPORATION that lays stress on respecting human nature possesses an ethos and a climate of emphasizing the indispensable aspects of human life.

What really supports our society is not what constitutes the beautifully ornamented, gorgeous surface mask, but what nobody wants to touch or be involved with: the disposal of waste — human, household, corporate, and industrial. We prefer to eat food that has been made pleasing to the eye in addition to being tasty. Recently, the interest in fine food seems to have grown exponentially. Expertise and an industry that can respond accordingly are necessary for our society and look to be very promising fields with high growth potential.

However, we should not forget that one of our essential bodily functions is to excrete the beautiful food that we eat. Should we be equally enthusiastic about the act of eating and the disposal of excrement? Rather, it is here that the indispensability of both elements and their value to society must be acknowledged, in turn fostering an ethos of greater respect for people participating in such basic cleanup and support work.

Those occupations that support the fundamentals of human life — agriculture, the fishing industry, etc. — are neither physically nor economically easy. If the general dis- position of society is to look down upon people engaged in this kind of labor, and rather to respect "men of many words," our world will become one where the numbers of those who support our lives will decrease, while others seek only work that is pleasant and enjoys respect.

disposition of no処理 [handwritten annotation]

In an organization, who is more important, the "thinker" or the leader of the working group? They are both important; however, it is imperative that the thinker avoids being ranked higher or making decisions. At all times, all decisions and orders should come from the leader, with supporting opinions being supplied by the thinker. The important thing for the thinker is not to exceed the position, nor for the leader to allow the position to be exceeded.

The working group in a company is consistently given respectful priority. Even so, work does not proceed through words alone. Thus, it is vital to foster a company tradition that focuses attention on taking the initiative in carrying out work that others may shy away from, entrusting staff with executive power, and on implementation.

If we say that society has become a knowledge society and that now is the age of the knowledge industry, we tend to value the planner and the strategist higher than the executor. However, this is thinking that does not discern the real nature of knowledge. A distinction needs to be made between information and knowledge. Information is where something is simply conveyed to us; knowledge means the experience gained from the results of actually putting information into practice. Thus, knowledge is something that can be acquired through the experiencing of information.

Therefore, the more society becomes a knowledge society, the less it values simply obtaining or parroting information. The key lies in the accumulation of actual experience through utilizing information in practice, seeing, and then reflecting upon the results.

For "human evaluation" in a company, priority should be placed on application and the person who carries out tasks should be highly evaluated. Anything that a company with a weak working group tries to implement cannot possibly be successful. However, to attempt to stimulate energy by arousing ambition is not a desirable way of managing. Furiously arousing ambitious desire by dangling carrots of substantial reward (difficult to obtain) in front of employees as an incentive deserves to be condemned as the most derisive kind of act.

Then, where is human dignity to be found? Trifling with desires, which can also be termed people's feelings (often difficult to control and an acknowledged weakness of humans), is a serious error. This kind of conduct is certain to both ruin human relations and give rise to conflict, because ambition is limitless and its needs will rapidly become difficult to satisfy. However, because the working relationship between the two sides is based upon deepening ambition and responding to it, the moment this collapses, inhuman aspects will be revealed that cause dispute. Therefore, management should not recklessly flaunt difficult-to-obtain rewards in order to elicit desire. A low level of human relations should not be sought and employees' normal feelings should never be ignored or dismissed, but rather, efforts should be made to create an atmosphere of human relations where employees may find happiness in spiritual fulfillment.

In this way, the company will be filled with a peaceful yet dynamic harmony, in which the feeling of gratitude and

TAO Management

the pleasure of "voluntary" ambition will be at play in a pervasive atmosphere of ease and mutual respect.

No. 4 MU-GEN

Substance and Firmness
Form the Basis

WHEN THE MIND IS FILLED with some degree of anxiety, even if there are other things to think about, concentration is impossible and thinking cannot be achieved. Becoming full and/or making full are thus not necessarily positive qualities. When a toy balloon is filled to its limit with air, bursting is the only thing that can happen next. Once it is fully expanded, the rubber stretches and breaks and there is no return to the original condition; the true form is wrecked.

In corporate management as well, investing all resources to the limit will mean that even if everything goes well at first, things will not continue in this way. There is also the danger of great damage being done to the original form. A situation of emptiness is one where most energy is produced. When the head is full of worries, when the stomach is so full that one cannot move, human energy is completely stifled. When we think about a mind that is clear and unfettered or a body in a buoyant state, it is easy to understand that "emptiness" is desirable.

For humans, is acumen needed above everything else? At times it bears down on others causing great pain. One who has been hurt will often fight back, giving rise to the creation of dispute. If corporate activities are narrowly focused on shrewdness for the sake of conquering the market, the company will rapidly try to thrust itself into gaps left by other companies. Such conduct will likely prompt the contraction of other companies' activities while inviting their fierce counterattacks, resulting in a forced, unnecessary conflict.

Acumen is fragile. If it is excessive, weakness occurs causing easy breakage. Again, the too gaudy, the too showy are not desirable qualities. If the activity of the corporation is too flamboyant, it will invite jealousy that, when incurred, becomes an impediment to smooth progress. Thus, the company should always be looking at whether its activities are conducted too acutely, too conspicuously, or too flamboyantly. It is important to monitor one's company by constantly keeping an eye on the response of the general public and strive to be seen from and be responsive to the perspective of ordinary people. If paying this kind of attention is an ongoing process, the company itself will become one supported by a solid and stable base, whose activities are neither merely superficial nor overly conspicuous but firm and reliable, conducted soundly, and with a natural quality.

# No. 5 KYO-YOH

The Energy of Creation Pours Out

THE UNIVERSE HAS NO SPECIAL FEELINGS; nor does it have what we call affection. Rather, it has an impartial, extremely natural attitude that humans should also adopt as their ideal.

The ideal form of human relations is not one where we approach everyone with strong affection in our minds. If we do not harbor any special feelings, do not carry love in our minds when we make contact with others, neither will we carry enmity with us in our associations. We must adopt an identical attitude towards everyone and embrace a steadfast spirit in all our associations. Thus, there is no special person, no special care; and there are no particular favorites in our relations. If there is no partiality, neither is there an attitude of indifferent heartlessness. No matter what kind of other party is involved, the same evenness will be maintained.

An enterprise is a group comprised of human beings, and various relationships are constantly being formed and dissolved that incorporate the full range of human feelings.

This emotional energy may reach immeasurable proportions, and, in the worst case, cause the formation of cliques engaged in a power struggle that may eventually lead to the company's impoverishment. As it fiercely expands, the energy of negative feeling emanating from such a conflicted human group envelops not only the members themselves, but also those on the outside, such as suppliers and client companies, rapidly compounding its negative impact. Once this kind of energy occurs, if considerable strength is not exercised to suppress it by drastically replacing members, it will invariably flare up when not expected. Why does this happen? There is only one reason. The leader's or top management's attitude lacks the even-mindedness requisite to implement the work at hand. Special feelings should not be directed towards one's subordinates, but the association should be made with an evenness of attitude and a consistency of words and deeds. Associations with one's peers and upper management should also respectfully reflect this approach. This means not a trace of strong, special feeling for any individual. Thus, neither is there any opposite feeling of hatred or heartlessness.

We are sometimes told that human feeling is an essential element of leadership, but this is far from the truth. Some subordinates will then be shown kindness while others will not, and from the receiving end, the subordinate may feel let down or greatly disappointed, and perhaps even an intense hatred. Therefore, right from the start, it is better if there is no special human feeling. The kind of attitude management should adopt is one where relationships are made from an unchanging, disinterested stance.

The reason why the universe continuously gives birth to an infinite number of things is that the space of the universe, just as that in a pair of bellows, is an emptiness containing nothing. Inside the bellows is not filled with air but is always empty so that it can suck in air and then expel it. This is the essence of creativity.

Thus, in business, if a stream of various products of worth is to be provided to society and the market, success will hinge on keeping the heads of those in charge empty. What does this mean? It means banishing established concepts, abandoning the limitations of past common sense and experience, and starting each day freshly and with excitement, especially when engaged in experimentation or development. In this way, what was overlooked because of being thought absurd and discoveries that defied explanation based upon past experience can be captured, resulting in commodities that have never before existed. Research and development institutes that have an abundance of past successes are hampered the most. The past should be recognized as such, and when success has been achieved, the pattern of development should be absorbed as having the potential for wide application while realizing that some day it could also become an obstacle. That is, it should be completely set aside as one starts freshly from zero.

Rather than being a slave of the past, human beings should welcome each morning as a completely new, blank canvas. If we are open to being surprised and if we experience each day freshly, a new creative energy will emerge from our inner depths.

No. 6 SEI-SHO

Energy from Society

THE TAO, THE ORIGIN OF THE COSMOS that gave birth to everything in this world, is unceasing and eternal, never showing tiredness as it continues to create myriads of things.

Likewise, a business may have no end, and must continuously bear social responsibility because bankruptcy, here considered as the opposite of continuity, is a betrayal of the investors, stockholders, and others involved. There is little use in merely existing, so the company should develop and continuously strive to fulfill its potential. To best learn how to be and practically how to do business as a company, it is necessary to inherit the essence and function of the originator of the universe, the Tao, and adopt its fundamental principles. The Tao is never-ending and eternal because it is involved only in the creation of things and does not make any appeals about its own existence, nor does it try to impress, so there is no wastage of energy.

The creation of things in itself, when it enters the cycle of cosmic energy and is in tune with it, shows no tiredness. Rather, when things are created, this causes a cycle of vigorous ongoing action so there is always an intake of new energy and thus no aging or decline.

For what purpose does an enterprise exist? It is to change society and our lives for the better. To make our lives more convenient, more comfortable, richer, more enjoyable, and/or healthier, a company offers attractive social proposals. In their concrete form, these are expressed as business, products, and services. Resting upon this meaning only, there is never any self-appeal or proclivity towards being conspicuous. The sole purpose of corporate activity is to make significant contributions to society, and its success hinges on precisely what kind of attractive business, products, and services it can present. No claims are made for the company itself as the whole meaning of the company resides in its offerings.

When members of society like, express their thanks for, and highly value something that has been provided, a flow of positive energy will return from the whole of society itself. The company will readily absorb this new energy with the result that more splendid, high-value business, products, and services will be provided. Will such a company face decline? Is there any danger of collapse?

Making appeals for the company itself does not in any way contribute to society and so society will not reciprocate. It merely causes waste that results in tiredness and consequent a loss of energy. This is a most important point, and well worth remembering.

The Eternal Cycle

A S THE UNIVERSE IN WHICH WE LIVE continues un-ceasingly to create a vast number of things, we can say that it is everlasting. Why has it continued for so long? It is because it does not itself try to stay alive. What can this mean? When we put all our hearts into our work, do we do so with the thought of it continuing for a long time? No, rather, we focus upon the task at hand. Thus, the relationship between people and work goes on with little regard for the continuity of one's present position and situation, as one is devoted to the job itself.

Corporate business is not carried out for the sake of continuing the company. Work is done because it is work that the company wants most to do. The real gratification may be gained when one is tackling or struggling with a given task. In concentrating and feeling excitement, as well as being profoundly engaged through one's interest, pleasure is thus felt in being in contact with the job itself.

There is little happiness to be gained from simply continuing something. The true feeling of existence is not in continuity alone but in being engaged in work. Why do we work? Why do we manage companies? Because we can deeply feel our sense of existence in doing so. Through this, we have already achieved our aim: a deep feeling of our sense of existence and a feeling of pleasure. Surely this is enough.

The work itself must be tackled wholeheartedly because we want to feel the wonderful, ultimate sensation of being alive. Results will follow later. If results are sought and even if work is carried out to preserve continuity, it is not guaranteed that this will actually happen and often does not. There is only one essential point in ensuring continuity: never losing interest and enthusiasm in one's work. Consequently, "a new challenge" is a vital element and constant challenge will ensure that interest in one's work is maintained. Thus, a company that loses passion for its business cannot hope to continue.

For the creation of better products, the only method to ensure that interest and passion are not lost is to raise one's aims by continuously challenging higher level, unexplored territories. This is why entering new fields is also of vital importance. However, it is not for the purpose of the company's continuation. If new work is approached with this view, harmony will be lost because the new field will come first while the interest and spirit of challenge of those who work there will be merely an afterthought and result in an unnatural situation where time is wasted in constructing agreement between aims and desires. Entering a new field is for the purpose of maintaining interest and enthusiasm, and so new fields aiming for the expression of interest and passion should be introduced, entered, and explored.

The company that feels the practice of corporate business itself is meaningful will pay close attention to the carrying out of that work and all its energy will be so invested. The reputation of the company itself, as well as of its president, will be recognized as being completely outside the required aims. Therefore, the energy spent on these kinds of things will be focused only upon corporate business, or be invested in systems and facilities enabling all workers to devote themselves to company business. Consideration will also be given to things that allow workers to continue bringing interest and passion to their jobs: i.e., a support system that addresses various family problems or a counseling system. This in turn will facilitate the ongoing provision of products and services to society into which workers have put their passion and desire — in other words, energy. Due to the present scarcity of such sound products, they will be greatly welcomed by society. That is, something of value will be given to society and so something of value will be returned by society. This kind of company will not suffer from decline; its continuity will manifest itself in a very natural way.

Why will this be so? Because corporate business is not seen from the point of view of permanency, prosperity, and profit making. Self-interest does not give birth to a flow of energy, nor is a sympathetic relationship with society formed. Let us assume that things have gone unexpectedly well. It is good if the company continues for even ten years, but this is far from permanency. Having said that, isn't it acceptable if a social contribution has been made? The truth is that a mutually beneficial relationship with society has not been realized. The satisfaction of engaging in activities that contribute to society has had the effect of minimizing the concentration that goes into the developing and manufacturing of products, with the result that providing something of value runs out of steam.

One person meets another and they decide to form a company because they want to change and improve society and the lives of human beings. The company staff basically want to carry out the business of the company, so the workers will put their hearts into the job. Eventually, they will have to assume a broader societal role and will thus become more essential to society. As all workers will devote themselves to carrying out work that they themselves actually want to do and, because they will continuously challenge higher aims, the workers' interest will not wane. Because better and better high-quality products will be continuously provided, society will make it even more necessary for such a company to exist. It is this that should be the relationship between society and business.

No. 8 EKI-SEI 易姓 (中国で, 王朝が代わること)

Goodness Is Like Water

IT IS WATER that offers us the finest kind of model to follow. Nothing else bestows as much benefit upon so many living things. There is no living thing on this earth that does not need water — plants, animals, and humans alike. Its existence is indispensable.

Even though water is so precious, it is not assertive in itself. If it is put into a circular receptacle, it becomes circular; into a square one, it becomes square. It is free and unrestricted, never in dispute with anything it comes into contact with, and even changes its shape to fit those things. It is so free that it does not have an original shape of its own.

Water flows down into lower positions that are disliked by many people; it never tries to rise up to a higher place. "Rain wears even the stone," as it can open up holes in the most solid of rocks. It can also become a raging torrent, possessing the power to sweep everything away. Water is the ideal said to be closest to the essence of the Tao. We would be wise to adopt it as a model to follow in life as well as in the corporate world.

In business, we should learn the "mentality of non-dispute" from water: while being irreplaceable, never engaging in conflict. Further, in the same way that water quenches the thirst of a dry throat, the company must define what kind of thirst it will attempt to satisfy for a large number of people. It could be in making something taste delicious, or in quenching a thirsty mind.

Because people's thirst for something can be relieved, the company then becomes essential for those people. However, even though the company is necessary and important, customers should be approached with an attitude of modesty and humility. Their needs must be met like water, as every effort must be made to determine how one can adapt to fit. Where a dispute is apt to occur in resolving complaints, and even in cases of disputes themselves, one should not rigidly hold to one's own views, but should try to deal with the situation by reaching agreement with the customer's claims and opinions. If this is done, the danger of disputes that can easily happen between the two sides will disappear, and the relationship will become congenial like that of parent and child, like siblings or colleagues, thus leading to the most favorable solution for each side.

If the dispute deepens, no solutions will be found. The company must first show humility and be prepared not to confront but to listen to the customer. Based upon humility that stems from the confidence of being professional, avoiding dispute and aligning with the customer's view will then allow the company to unfailingly take the lead.

To learn more from water, consider its perseverance in making a hole in a rock over a long period of time. It never gives up and values the worth of continuing even drop by drop. For business, there is nothing so necessary as power, and this too must be learned from water. Where does the power of water come from? Imagine a situation of silent, still water. To make the water flow rapidly it must first be made to move. Nothing will be produced without movement.

TAO Management

Next, there must be simultaneous and congruent flow. To implement this process in a corporate setting, in line with the aims of the entire company, its focus of intent should be determined and unified while planning functions to generate the necessary power. The most important thing is to accumulate energy. The discharge of instantaneously produced energy results in a depletion of energy. Consideration must always be given to achieve a constant balance between accumulation and discharge, while it is vital that a consistent amount of reserve power is maintained.

Characteristics of the ideal situation can also be learned from water. The best kind of situation is one of "peace and quiet," which comes from "symbiotic non-dispute." The movement of flowing water, as well as its own natural action, causes the absorption of extracts from minerals and plants the water touches, bringing about a richness of content. There should be no rejection or denial of this kind of contact. The basic mentality that amalgamates and blends diverse elements should be adopted by an enterprise. This kind of company will always synthesize what it extracts from the personnel it comes into contact with and may even bring them into its organization. It is the same with expertise, equipment, funds, and know-how.

Indeed, the fusion of all things contacted is a source that enriches the company to an immeasurable extent. When water is supplied to plants it makes them grow. A huge number of fish are also raised because of water. Similarly, it is not merely a case of mutual partnership but one where growth is actually fostered. The fundamental role of a company is not only to look after its own workers, but also to foster the growth of those outside the company with whom it has connections, even including the customer. Thus, the energy generated by those taken care of by the company will in turn serve as a source of growth of the company itself.

Basically, the company that embraces the concept of water will try to provide things indispensable to people. It will always work in partnership with its customers with not the slightest sign of a confrontational attitude. Therefore, it does not recklessly broadcast its own virtues.

Everything depends on the people who have connections with the company. By applying their virtues and strong points to company business, the potential of the company can be raised still further. In turn, the people so utilized will be given a place to allow them to develop, to exercise, and to display their abilities. Further, no matter how impossible something may seem, it will be challenged in a spirit of determined perseverance. Thus, the impossible will eventually be made possible, leading to a more valuable contribution to society. Sometimes, like water in a swift current or from a waterfall, or the gushing water after a heavy downpour, an unstoppable energy will be generated, ensuring the ongoing achievement of one's aims.

Room — The Key to Growth

WHEN SOMETHING IS FILLED TO ITS LIMIT with no breathing space and no room to maneuver, this is the worst kind of situation. What happens when we try to carry a cup filled to the brim with water? To prevent spillage, the body cannot move as it would wish and even taking a step forward is not an easy task. In this way, even one cup filled with water robs the body of its freedom.

Equally, a blade that has been sharpened to its limit will become weak, lose its sharpness, and become brittle. Thus, if something is sharply developed to its limit, it will, contrarily, become weak and lose its durability.

In the case of food, when the stomach is completely full, the value and flavor of food are lost and a feeling of discomfort results wherein the body itself finds it difficult to move. The reason why "fullness" or "full to capacity" are not desirable is that the potential of the receptacle will be stifled. When the stomach is full, its functionality and that of the digestive organs will be suppressed, resulting in a feeling of heaviness and perhaps even damage.

It is the same in a company. If at the customer's request, sales of products are maximized, the company will be forced to work to the limit of its capacity. This, in turn, will cause mistakes or losses leading to not only disappointment for the client, but also to a severe decline in the company's capabilities. The situation will become one where it is all that the company can do to finish off current work, and so there will be no leeway to even attempt to develop and then to provide products of better value. Eventually, the company's condition will sink to a level where it will not in any way be able to supply products that can satisfy the client.

In a sense, the company resembles what the stomach is to food. When something has to be digested and the stomach is at its bursting point, even simple movement becomes impossible. But, because the effort to assimilate continues, a complete breakdown of functional ability itself occurs. If this analogy is adopted, just because goods can be sold does not justify maximum manufacturing and selling. The company must recognize its own capabilities, limiting its orders to 70 percent or 80 percent of its capacity, focusing meanwhile on maintaining a constant level of quality and service for each of its products. In cases where orders cannot be met, the company has to explain the reason honestly and ask the client to wait.

If this is done, there will always be something held in reserve not only to support the growth of the company's abilities, but also to maintain high quality. To further improve service, a system of securing orders through advance payment can be established so that payment will have been collected before manufacturing of the products begins. Compared to collecting money through a billing process, there will be a huge (and positive) difference in the profit margin. Keeping orders to 70 or 80 percent will allow both company policy and operations to focus on maintaining high quality and developing products of high value. Personnel values will be shaped not towards flippancy or intoxication with a flash-in-the-pan explosion of high corporate achievement, but rather a sound corporate climate of composure and dignity will be established.

An enterprise never ends. If continuation is considered as being the life of the company, the disparity in the nature of this kind of climate is very important. If one's energy is consumed to its limit, naturally time will be needed for recovery during which the consumption of energy has to be avoided. If even a small amount of energy is continuously consumed in this period, too, one's body will suffer injury and may even sustain damage beyond recovery.

In corporate activity, there is no recovery period. The supply of energy must be quietly constant and there is no time to suspend operations. As a rule, company activities must be continued 365 days a year without a break. From this perspective, the most important thing for corporate activity is to determine how to carry out its business without having the need for down time to recover its energy. It is this that constitutes management where orders are kept to within 70 or 80 percent, leaving energy for tomorrow, and consistently allowing a leeway. A "modest attitude" is necessary for the same reasons.

As the wealth of the company increases, why shouldn't this be a cause of pride? Why should there be a retreat when success and reputation have been achieved? Wealth and success are signs of a situation approaching the limit. That does not mean to say that wealth and success are all bad: they are, indeed, part of how things should be. Rather, they serve as indicators of a state where it is necessary to return to a situation of 70 or 80 percent. This return itself is modesty, and when this is achieved, it will naturally provide leeway and allow for the creation of further vitality. Thus, the possibility of yet greater advancement will appear.

 **No. 10 NOH-I**

Separating Life and Death

HUMAN BEINGS ARE KEPT ALIVE by blood and respiration. So the more we want to intensify our vitality, the more important it is for these two elements to be not separated, but to perform in unison. They work separately where there is some disturbance or agitation — in times of anger, fear, sadness, or astonishment — or when there is some risk to life. Vitality is powerfully expressed in contrasting times when the mind is in a state of peace and tranquility.

How can this situation of calm be achieved? The answer is to trust in and live in a state of togetherness with the Tao, the powerful origin of everything on this earth. Being at one with the Tao is indeed the source of vitality, and to achieve this, there should be no doubt about its existence. At times there is a dialogue, at times one feels its breath, thus naturally feeling the existence of the Tao. Even momentarily, it should not be forgotten that union with the Tao is the basis of life. Thus, no matter what is about to happen, remembering this connection will result in a state where the mind is always kept calm, and this tranquility will lead to an even more intensified feeling of togetherness with the Tao. When this happens, blood begins to flow vigorously, breathing becomes deep and slow, and a flow of energy rises and begins to circulate, bringing about an even stronger vitality. This is exactly like an infant sleeping in its mother's arms: it is so light that, even though there is bodily flesh, it is as if no attention is paid to this and the mind becomes detached. It is in this state of detachment where the greatest amount of energy is strongly and smoothly released. It is precisely this detachment that, in combination with one's five senses, brings into play a sixth sense that produces the ability to see that which cannot be seen and allows for the realization of absolute truth.

If one wants to know something, the answer will always be forthcoming. Since it will be enough to know only what is necessary, not knowing most things will have no adverse effect.

In corporate activity, too, because the flow of funds, which is equivalent to the flow of blood, the flow of values, which is equivalent to breathing, and the flow of air will all unite and circulate smoothly, the energy of the company will be ever ongoing and tirelessly produced.

What is the source of this energy? It lies in unity with the Tao, or in other words, the execution of business in a state of detachment. Pride in contributing to the advancement of society and our lives, creating high value, having the desire to challenge the next task, and satisfaction will follow. More precisely, it is the clarity and satisfaction obtained only within companies that continuously proceed in this correct direction that strengthens one's feeling of unity with the Tao.

Even though the Tao has given birth to so many things, it does not claim exclusive ownership and though so many things have been achieved, the Tao does not expect any reward. It is responsible for the growth of many things, but in fostering this growth it does not dominate these things. This is its very essence. Creating things, putting ideas into practice, and fostering growth and development are truly necessary and as natural as it is to grow and develop. To have private possession of, self-interest in, and to exercise domination of this success and development runs contrary to reason and nature.

Why should this be so? The essence of the Tao does not lie in possession and preservation, but in creating things, carrying out tasks, and promoting growth, achievement, and development. So our objective should be to devote ourselves to equivalent challenges with enthusiasm and excitement, in turn leading to a profound feeling of satisfaction. The point is not what kind of wealth or power has been accumulated, or what kind of status has been achieved, but how splendid, how fulfilling each moment of life is. The proof of this is that when we die, we have to abandon everything: we are born as one body; we die as one body. Life is how we spend each and every moment.

見えないところが見える人

No. 11 MU-YOH 無用

Because Something Invisible Exists

WHEN WE SEE, we usually try to look only at what is actually there in front of us. Should we try to see not only visible but also invisible things? Yes, and further, we should try to be aware of what does not tangibly exist, try to see it, and recognize its worth. For example, a house exists for the very reason that it consists of spaces, or the rooms of the house. Thus, not so much attention should be paid to how good and how well-made the elements are that form the shape of the house — the pillars and walls, the doors and windows, the ceilings and the floors — but, primarily, we should focus on the existence of the spaces created by these elements. It is the empty space that gives the room meaning. The same can be said for receptacles. A teacup has space into which tea can be poured, and it is precisely this that allows the teacup to perform its function. In the case of a chest of drawers, because there is space, clothes and other things can be put into it. We should therefore focus our attention towards space: how easily it can accommodate

things and to what degree of comfort it has been filled or used. In this way, that which exists brings out the value of that which does not. Concurrently, it is the function of that which does not exist that confirms the existence of that which is. Thus, the Tao cannot be seen or touched, but its majestic presence is the force responsible for the existence of a vast multitude of things. It is necessary for us to embrace the nothingness of the Tao from that which is.

In a company, the elements that cannot be seen are especially important, so the secret of management lies in how the unseen elements are seen and dealt with. The principal invisible element is the climate of the company. This is something that develops over time and, when firmly established after two or three years, imparts a certain uniform set of rules and common sense to subsequent company staff, with the result that the workers' thoughts and actions are encompassed within this invisible net.

The greatest impetus given towards creating the corporate climate comes from the company's Number 2 person because the Number 2 occupies the highest position that has a superior. In every action carried out within the company, as well as in learning how to deal with things in general, one inevitably has to rely on a more experienced person as a model, and when one goes in search of further models, one comes to the Number 2. The president is the only person who has no one above and so cannot be relied upon as a model. The Number 2's every action towards the president, and his or her method of dealing with everything, thus becomes the example for all staff to follow. The Number 2, therefore, is a person of vital importance for a company. Should the company be so unfortunate as to have a Number 2 who presents a false sense of obedience in his or her style of work, then this will also become the basis of the company's climate. It is the same in the case of a family: the mother's attitude towards her husband forms the atmosphere in the home. The persons in this kind of position —

the mother or the Number 2 — must be cognizant of this and should pay close attention to their style of conduct as they will be treated in the same way by the Number 3.

Another important point regarding elements that cannot be seen in a company is how to handle "Invisible Expenditure." What is required to be an excellent leader? It is the ability to see invisible parts. Thus, the ability to perceive signs of what is going to happen tomorrow or the day after tomorrow, as well as the ability to see clearly what is happening beneath the surface, what is done at each employee's discretion and kept secret from the organization, and that which nobody notices or is routinely overlooked is crucial.

The company's earnings, without understanding why and in some obscure way, may again depart, so it is more important than one may think to keep a check on points of expenditure. The collapse of an organization has often been caused by its leader not being able to perceive a large number of elements. That a leader exists who can also see the unseen parts will continually impart a sense of alertness that will result in a retention of enthusiasm for each facet of work to be carried out. In other words, it is precisely this policy of tightening up of the unseen that tightens up that which can be seen. Thus, in this way, the majority of elements of an enterprise are formed by the smooth and beneficial development of the action of its unseen parts. Our lives proceed in the same way.

No. 12 KEN-YOKU 謙抑 ?

The Company's Sense of Joy in Being Alive

WHERE IS OUR <u>NATURAL, TRUE JOY TO BE FOUND?</u> What is it that <u>moves us so profoundly?</u> Is it the beauty of color, of music, or perhaps attractive, delicious food? It is true that the greater the number of fine works produced by masters, the greater is our satisfaction and delight, but, is this really the ultimate feeling of joy and deep pleasure? In fact, it is not so. There is a limit to this kind of <u>material and external satisfaction.</u> Rather, <u>the joy and profound sense of happiness that envelops one's whole being are to be found</u> in something simpler — in the deep interior of our hearts. What about the moment of delight felt when one is at last able to do something that took a long time to achieve? Or the sense of pleasure when one has finally and successfully solved a nagging problem? Or when, behind us, we feel the <u>guiding presence of the Tao acting as</u> if to protect us, or in other words, <u>the moment of profound joy</u> when we feel life's truth? The full extent of this kind of joy and deep pleasure are on a scale that defies expression. Nothing compares with that moment of joy experienced as the feeling of, "I am alive!" When we read how people who have intimately felt the presence of death due to incurable illness or those who have come back from the brink of death have eulogized the "joy of being alive," we inevitably notice an elemental simplicity in their writing. From the writer, Yasushi Inoue, shortly before his death:

All day I sit upright
my face towards the garden.
The trees, the sky, the clouds, the wind,
the birds are all alive, quietly alive.
The sun's rays and the sound of distant bicycles
also are all alive.
In the midst of all living things
sitting in a corner of my study
I too am alive.

True joy comes from the joy of being alive. It is felt everywhere, even in the most commonplace and plainest of surroundings. When this happens, the surroundings undergo a complete change, taking on a rare brilliance and imparting the finest of messages to us. Ironically, as we get more attracted by ornamentation such as the beautiful colors of clothing, accessories, and jewelry, our sense of feeling true joy is lost. The same holds true for fine music and impeccably presented, delicious food as our senses of seeing, hearing, and taste become clouded.

Desire has the character of "no limitation." In other words, limitation seems to disappear once the fulfillment of desire is pursued. Indispensable for us and with a tremendous inherent power to create energy, it is not something to be abhorred but rather to be made use of, and used wisely can bring huge benefits to society. Desire, though, is like an untamed horse or a double-edged sword. If the situation becomes one where control is lost, there is a strong, inherent power that can take away human life. Thus, it is best kept

いとわ
きらう

野性の
馬

両刃（もろ刃）の剣

本来備わっている

carefully under control. However, it may be most fruitfully used in elucidating that which is obscure, i.e., human's search for truth, as well as focused towards developing ideas and technology that will benefit society. While doing so, one should cultivate a state of mind in which to feel the joys of living a simple and ordinary life.

An enterprise is something where attractive social proposals are carried out for the beneficial transformation of society and our lives. If a company tries to alleviate, even to a small extent, the inconveniences and discomforts of human society, the people working there can feel healthy joy in working together for the sake of other human beings. To be able to feel such joy as well as experience kindness and attention from a fellow worker, each person's desire should be discreetly controlled and management should be carried out with an emphasis on simplicity and truth.

Looking Inside Oneself

APERSON'S FEELINGS ARE TRIFLED WITH and she or he feels either joy or sorrow when receiving courteous or rude treatment. Can we call this our own life when we live in a state where someone else controls our feelings? The reason why this happens is that the fundamentals of life are based on relationships with others and not on oneself. Or else, they are based on materialism and to what extent one can acquire material things. How one is treated by others and how many material possessions one can acquire is not true happiness. Real happiness is the feeling of satisfaction within oneself such as when one's abilities are elevated, that which could not quite be achieved before becomes possible, that which could not be understood is mastered, and one is able to manage these things with complete freedom. Further, it is like the condition where one has become united with the power of the vast cosmos.

Always keep your criteria on a cosmic scale. Compared to the vastness of the cosmos, the world is tiny. A part of this world, Japan, is even smaller. In the middle of this, in Tokyo, your even more minute problems are insignificant.

We are all a part of the Tao that created this universe and is the source of all things within it. We should not forget that we are thus a part of this source of creation. As long as this is remembered, energy from the Tao will continue to be supplied.

In an enterprise, the greatest concern is placed on how the staff treats each other. The worst thing that can happen is when the majority of staff knows something that you do not, a situation where you are "left out." When this happens, even information that is not necessary is given to everyone anyway. On further escalation, before being given to everyone else, the information is given to you only, tacitly implying that there is no one as important as you, but also causing "maneuvering behind the scenes." This depicts but a mere fragment of all-too-common practice inside an enterprise. When seen from the point of view of the whole company, such energy expenditure is colossal. Living with excessive focus upon how one is treated in an organization is another reflection of this process.

What is truly good for one's body? What is it that really maintains our own sense of self-respect? Is it always surrounding oneself with wealth? Is it taking the finest food? Is it doing only what we like doing? Is it giving oneself up to pleasure? What really compels our respect is the striving for improvement of our own sense of humanity. What is this sense of human development?

The most necessary thing for a company is for all members to reach a level where they enjoy their work. It is very easy to spend all night playing mahjong or video games, but a company must get rid of those who do not feel the same way about their jobs. The reason why some people do not enjoy their jobs may be found in the answer to the question, "Were mahjong and video games enjoyable from the start?" At first, nothing is interesting. For something to become interesting, the ability to enjoy it is necessary, and then it becomes necessary to achieve a certain level of skill. What can be done to reach this level? Unless training is carried out with a certain intensity of rigor and discipline, this level will not be reached. This often necessitates working with an experienced coach, guide, or consultant, but more than anything else, it requires a spirit of challenge that does not チャレンジ精神 mind a little strictness. It is essential that a climate where the desire for challenge is never lost consistently pervades the company.

No. 14 SAN-GEN 三た元

The Invisible Will Be Seen

超える
しのぐ
にまさる

EVEN IF WE TRY TO SEE THE TAO we cannot. Even if we try to hear its voice we cannot. Even if we try to touch it we cannot. It is something that we cannot grasp with our usual human senses. In this way, because the Tao itself is difficult to comprehend, it is telling us the importance of understanding its essential truth by transcending rational and logical thinking, and thus advocating the necessity and importance of mastery through feeling and direct experience. Further, we can say that the existence of that which isn't brings about the formation of that which actually is. One example of this is that we can perceive sound because of the existence of a silent nothingness, an empty space. If sound were to continue forever, would we be able to hear it?

On a cosmic scale, the cosmos consists of that which does not exist and that which does, so all things can exist because of the nothingness of the Tao; or, it can also be said that because we exist, the nothingness of the Tao also exists. Thus, nothingness cannot be grasped using the same methods of seeing and hearing as where something exists. In other words, we cannot achieve understanding of the Tao through abilities whose usefulness is limited by the boundaries of our perception; this is precisely why transcendental, experiential understanding is required. As one seeks to open a way to the world where one can see the unseen and hear the unheard, classic Asian thought, which holds experiential understanding in high regard, has great richness to offer us now.

The more highly developed we become, the more we will be able to see the unseen, hear that which cannot be heard, and grasp that which we had found difficult to understand. To reach this kind of domain it is necessary to undergo "training" by devoting oneself to one's work. Thus, because work as a method of training is a way of achieving excellence, it does not matter what the work involves. If even a bank worker thinks about carrying out his or her work as training, or a salesperson is conscious of doing her or his selling as training, it will become training towards achieving excellence. The crux of the matter lies in whether or not they carry out their work from this stance.

What exactly is it when we say that the previously not seen will be seen? Product development veterans often cite the following kind of experience:

> In the process of product development a serious problem arises and whether it can be solved becomes a matter of utmost importance. Day after day the person involved thinks of nothing else until, finally, it is the day before the deadline. He or she spends a sleepless night continuously thinking about the problem until the appearance of the morning light; however, no good ideas are forthcoming. In despair, he or she thinks that one may as well give up.

Feeling that there is nothing left to do but to get the little rest possible, just at the moment one is about to fall asleep, suddenly an image flashes through one's mind. It is unmistakably the perfect image for the product; the problem has already been solved, and the perfect, completed product has appeared.

What does it mean when we say that the sounds that cannot be heard will be heard? After a problem has been grappled with, as if in a moment of blankness, there is a time when the relieved mind is at rest. At that time, a voice, someone's voice, can be heard. The voice begins to give us some wonderful key words for dealing with the problems. With ongoing training, this will not be such an unusual occurrence but will become an everyday thing. Human beings are endowed with this unfathomable, mysterious capacity and the purpose of life is the self-development of this kind of ability. We also possess the special skill of devoting ourselves to our work and becoming completely absorbed in it. "At this place (here), at this time (now)" is the reality given to us throughout our lives. Yesterday and today are beyond our control and it is in the "here and now" that is our only chance to demonstrate our abilities. That is why it is necessary to exert our utmost efforts at each moment. Being devoted to and being completely absorbed in carrying out that particular job at that particular time is the height of our efforts and a cardinal point of life. This draws us further to an ideal unity with the energy of the Cosmos, thus bringing about the situation where that which cannot be seen becomes clear, that which cannot be heard is heard, and that which cannot be grasped is grasped. It is also the time when we most feel a sense of fulfillment.

Everyone possesses this kind of ability. To excel in expressing it is an essential element in making life enjoyable as well as being the secret to leading a fulfilling life. Meanwhile in the corporate world, it is the company that has a large

number of this kind of staff that is a human group where
meaningful human existence is being achieved.

The Ideal Leader

THE TAO, OR THE IDEAL WAY OF THE TAO, is the model that humans should adopt, but what kind of person follows the way of the Tao? Understanding the Tao is difficult and so the person of virtue who follows the Tao also possesses a combination of elements that are not easy to comprehend, or in other words, is a person of profoundness. Among some of the classical Chinese philosophers, such profoundness is considered to be one of the most desirable human characteristics.

To say that a person is profound is also to say that one possesses a complex character made up of an astonishingly large number of subtle elements, and because many of these elements are displayed in various ways at particular times as conditions require, such a person cannot be completely defined in words. However, if words must be used, then this person has the following characteristics:

First, this is a person of great prudence, with almost no element of fearlessness and heroism, but rather, a sense of hesitation with all things. Because this person can also be said to be somewhat doubting in approach, there is little danger of mistakes made because of carelessness, which means that there are no apparent weak points.

Next, this is a watchful person. This comes from being in awe of one's surroundings. There is no such thing as something that is done only by oneself. This person thinks what she or he does is only accomplished with support from others and that ultimately, one is given life through the mercy of the Tao. Therefore one has a great enthusiasm in getting to know one's surroundings, other people beyond the present situation, and care is always taken about such things. So there is no leaking of information, and a constant connection with one's environment is maintained.

It would seem that a prudent and watchful person might have no power of action and lack motivation, but this is not so. It is precisely because there is an abundance of both that a prudent and watchful character is indispensable. We recognize the importance of this when we look at how heroes and leaders everywhere, of all eras, met their downfall.

However, if the degree of prudence is excessive, there is a danger of one's becoming timid or cowardly. Otherwise, there is an imposing dignity and/or imperturbable composure without signs of consternation. One indication of this is a high degree of politeness. Frankness is also important, but whenever the mark is overstepped, impoliteness will be the result. It is therefore vital that the necessary amount of politeness is always maintained. Unlike a person with too much dignity that tends to result in pretentious politeness, a prudent and watchful person carries human warmth like spring sunlight. Human warmth can be said to be affection that is felt because we are fellow human beings, but again is something caused by the next element, a character of simplicity. This is an attitude of responding to all things directly and with sincere effort, where there is no trace of showing off one's superficial appearance, but rather a sincerity and honesty in expressing the undisguised self. This comes naturally from putting aside one's narrow self-interest, selfish artificiality, and self-satisfaction, and from cultivating a selfless broadmindedness. What exactly do we mean by selfless broadmindedness? The key here is no pursuit for full satisfaction.

Thus, it means not regarding such things as "to the limit," "completely," "all, if it can be obtained," and "using up everything" as desirable, but always stopping at 70 percent. Always leaving a bit of a gap, a space, and already being satisfied is a crucial element for the follower of the Tao. One is always satisfied with one's present situation. Knowing that 70 percent is enough, there is always 30 percent in reserve of one's own and others' energy. Therefore, because recovery is easy, there is no defeat. And, because the idea of being satisfied with 70 percent will always pervade one's attitude, an abundance of vitality will consistently be maintained for future possibilities. There is no intention of using everything up and so a pervasive sense of stability exists as one's surplus energy is maintained as a resource, which in turn fosters the gaining of society's trust, as well as its further development. This state exemplifies how to be for an enterprise that is destined to keep running without a competitive goal.

No. 16 KI-KON

Calmness and Emptiness
Form the Basis

ALL THINGS IN THIS WORLD, from their birth until leaving this world, flow along predetermined paths during their existence. Everything created into this world through the Tao follows its fixed orbit, eventually turning around and returning to the Tao, to its source. This is a universal truth of the natural world. Being aware of this truth, carefully observing and embracing it, and using it as a basis in our dealings with all things is the secret of making everything proceed smoothly. Our lives are no exception; death means returning to the Tao, to the origin. After being born from the calmness of the Tao, you enter a phase of growth and live a life that becomes busier and busier. Then reaching a turning point, you enter a latter period of life that becomes quieter and more stable before returning to the calmness of the Tao at last.

The purpose of life is to learn, to achieve, and to enjoy. Humans are forever learning something new, fulfilling their given roles, and rejoicing at having achieved their goals.

When conditions necessitate changes in our lives, naturally we should also make changes in how to learn, achieve, and enjoy. After the turning point, the cardinal point of life is to use our deep understanding of this universal truth as a basis for, slowly but surely and without haste, enjoying our daily lives through fulfillment of our important roles on a broad scale.

The ideal of the Tao, the origin, is "Calmness." This means that the fundamental ideal of human life — a creation of the Tao — is also to be found in preserving calmness. While maintaining both physical and mental calmness, if another ideal of the Tao, "Emptiness," is embraced, union with the Tao will be achieved. In other words, a return to the Tao, to the origin, is achieved even while living. In doing this, the viewpoint of the Tao is obtained, and so the permanent immutability and the fundamental principle, the truth of this world can be seen. Because the truth becomes visible, in turn, everything can be seen. First, it will be realized that everything, like oneself, continuously follows the path of permanent immutability. Then, you start to feel closeness, sympathy, or even affection in relationships with others who are also following such an unavoidable life path.

Embracing this kind of nature leads to a tolerant mind even when dealing with strangers, and such tolerance breeds fairness towards all things. Fairness brings about the acquisition of regal virtues enabling this person to cope with the laws of nature. This becomes the ideal of Tao in not only sustaining longevity, but also ensuring that no life-threatening danger exists. Conversely, if this kind of truth is not grasped, the person who merely carries out his or her actions haphazardly will not only be impeding smooth progress, but will also be inviting dangers to life.

Primary importance should be placed upon the fact that calmness has the nature of the Tao. Indeed, its continuous preservation is the best method in taking a closer step towards the Tao. Returning to calmness means that the

TAO Management

mind is at rest, and a restful mind means that one can utilize a new way of looking at things and at oneself quietly and objectively, thus bringing about a tolerance towards everything. The situation where the mind is in agitation, or when it is chopping and changing, trying to deal with a myriad of things at once, demonstrates how far removed it is from the Tao nature and should be avoided at all costs.

Nor can a company avoid this path of permanent immutability. A process of establishment, development, eventual full growth, and then decline is followed. This is true in the enterprise, in work, and for products. For a company that has fulfillment and continuous development as its basic mission, at the point in time when it is realized that a period of growth has come in a life cycle, preparation is made for the next. Thus, in order to sustain a company's business, it is important to establish a number of life cycles, so that work that is always inviting periods of growth will provide an ongoing support of company business.

For business that is in a period of decline, a return to the source has been made, and the tree has withered and returned to its root. To encourage new growth, it will be helpful to look carefully at past company successes and analyze them with a sense of gratitude for the ways in which they have contributed to the company's prior business. New buds should be sought there, and in conjunction with the results of the data analysis, should develop into new shoots, or new business.

In enterprises whose histories are ongoing, their employees reflect these life cycles as new faces enter, support the company's affairs for many years, and then leave due to retirement. It should not be forgotten that an enterprise stands firm because of the accumulation of valuable experience from these employees' lives.

No. 17 JUN-PU

Human Groups as the Ideal

WHAT EXACTLY IS THE IDEAL HUMAN GROUP, the enterprise? It is one in which, after mutual consultation, the employees decide upon the goals and directions to be taken. Since the enterprise exists to improve society and our lives, its employees decide on attractive social proposals by consultation with each other. Next, plans are developed to best implement these social proposals. After that duties are allocated and the employees exert all their efforts to smoothly carry out their respective tasks. A human being's greatest happiness is being useful for the sake of others and realizing this. Thus, within the company, the more the employee specifically contributes to society through his or her work, the greater the joy that will be received. But what about the results of human tasks carried out where the employee feels joy and ones where the employee feels discontent and dissatisfaction? Naturally, a big difference is apparent. If there was no difference, the high level of the business itself could not be guaranteed. When the workplace and the employees are happy, the results will follow naturally — corporate results will be improved and, as a distribution of these results, employees' remuneration will also be satisfactory. Thus, there is great satisfaction for both the company itself and its employees.

Why is it that companies cannot consistently progress under these kinds of conditions? What kind of energy is necessary? Clearly, there is a need for unseen leadership. When we look at the essential underlying factor that influences a voluntary spirit in employees, we see that it is trust between colleagues. The best way of understanding this is when we observe the strongest sports team or the finest orchestra. There, human relationship is basically formed by a relationship of trust. Putting it another way, no matter how able the members are, no matter how professional they are, if there is a lot of distrust in relationships, combined and organized power will not result. So, what is a trusting relationship in an organization attributable to?

However vast the organization, a start must be made from the relationship between the two people occupying the top positions: the CEO and the COO. How this relationship functions determines everything from the overall climate of the organization to its strength. Then, what is the basis of the relationship between these two? It is gratitude and loyalty. The top person respects the number 2 as a person, while the number 2 is always truthful in recognition of the top person's attitude. The relationship of trust between the top two people will permeate throughout the entire organization and this will determine its actual state. The existence of the top person is inconspicuous in this kind of organization. He or she is not the driving force behind all planning and decisions. The members of the organization believe that they carry out everything because they want to. They are convinced that the biggest reason why everything goes well lies with them, and thus, progress continues.

The ideal situation is one where nobody thinks about, or even notices that it is indeed the top person who skillfully runs the organization. The company employees feel happy in believing that it is through their own efforts and/or their own ingenuity that they gain results, or in other words that they are fulfilling their roles completely. Concurrently, as they will have a strong sense of responsibility, they will be very aware that they must do their best again tomorrow. Thus, motivation will be generated voluntarily. To achieve this ideal situation in the organization, the top person must: create an environment where employees can work comfortably, make it easy for employees to achieve better results, and create a situation where the strength of the organization can be brought into play. Succinctly, it is the arrangement of the surrounding environment that is the crucial role of the top person. As this is not something that the employees can clearly see, so the existence of the top person is vague to them. This is invisible leadership.

The word "organization" has been extensively used so far, but its use should not be limited to connection with enterprises only; it is also applicable to the family and other human associations. A second-rate top person can count on his or her employees to merely have pride in being friendly with him or her, one who is third-rate is feared by his or her employees, and one who is despised by his or her employees is simply out of the question. This is so because the sense of trust is thin, and this results from the fact that there is no attitude that, come what may, promises will be kept.

TAO Management

No. 18 ZOKU-HAKU

Great Harmony

WE HUMANS WERE CREATED BY THE TAO, the source of the cosmos. As the parent of all things born into this world, everything in this world happens within the actions of the Tao. Thus, the essence of the Tao is a model for us about how to lead our lives and there is nothing that does not proceed smoothly when carried out accordingly. The basis of the essence of the Tao is formed by calmness and emptiness. The mind is always kept tranquil and empty, unhampered and free. Moreover, the mind is kept open in its attitude towards others and other things because of the sympathy felt that one lives under the same circumstances.

TAO

But what happens when the Tao declines as a model in our lives? The result is the appearance of Jingi, or benevolence and morality, which is not the best kind of situation or kind of society. While the truth of the Tao is alive as the norm in this world, there is no need to preach Jingi or pay attention to it. We live for the sake of realizing the ideal society at its best, and it is precisely here that the ultimate goal is the Tao. A big reason why the Tao falls into disuse is because of paying excessive respect to those who are intelligent. In the distant past, there was an ideal society on this earth. People possessed a pure spirit, without self-interest or artificiality, rejected excess, and pooled their efforts in enjoying their days leading simple, peaceful lives cultivating fields, with filling the stomach as their greatest satisfaction. This is how we were — our way of life putting simplicity and quality first — in the olden days. When we look at who it was that brought artificiality, superficiality, and an ambition to outdo others into this kind of society, going from mutualism to competition, from unsophisticatedness to eloquence, and turned values upside down, it was the so-called person of intelligence. According to the essence of the Tao, the kind of wisdom advocated by these people is falsehood, and it should be remembered that it is a gross misdeed leading to turmoil in human society.

The origin of human society is the man/woman pair, the couple. With the birth of a child the parent/child relationship begins, and more children lead to sibling relationships. In the couple, parent/child, and sibling relationships, each "six blood relationship" is held together by strong bonds and built on mutual trust, foundations for a sound society. If the harmony of these kinds of relationships is broken, society flounders. Thus, the origin of politics is to be found in maintaining the harmony of this "six blood relationship." Special praise given to filial piety is done only because it is not something that happens very naturally. It is the same for a nation. If prominence is given to loyal subjects it only goes to show how few there are and is evidence that the society is not in harmony.

As a standard for measuring the level of organizational strength in an enterprise, one should look beyond praising employees for their efforts and devotion and inquire whether such factors are lacking in the organization as a whole. In the enterprise that has achieved a high level as an organization, there are no employees who need special

TAO Management

praise because all of them carry out their work perfectly as a matter of course.

The Tao has harmony as one of its qualities. When we look at the cosmos in general or a specific natural landscape, we have a deep feeling of the delicate harmony that goes into their formation. We can also feel that it is harmony itself that creates richness and tranquility. In relationships between humans as well, when we are in a relationship of mutual understanding and cooperation, it means that we are also in a situation where our mutual feelings are in harmony.

The leadership of the Tao is what prevents chaos and conflict and maintains constant order in the universe, and this leadership is harmony. Hence, the Tao is called "The Great Harmony." When the human spirit retains the sense of calmness and emptiness, eventually unity with the Tao will be felt, or in other words, harmony with the Tao will have been achieved. When this happens, a mixture of feelings such as gratitude, joy, and affection will well up from the depths of one's soul. This indeed is the true feeling of love with which we have been endowed. Without forgetting this feeling while we think of others in our relationships, there will be no dispute or discord, and absolutely no occurrence of such things as war.

TAO

No. 19 KAN

Enjoying Life

EVERYTHING IS INHERENT IN HUMANS. Especially when there is unity with the Tao, and the energy of the Cosmos is centered upon oneself, the fundamental condition of "enjoying life" is achieved. But why is it that this does not happen and frequently there is anxiety, suffering, disruption, and conflict with others? The reason is that we forget to show our true nature. Why do we forget? Because we put ourselves at the mercy of superficial, hypocritical objectives. What is this superficial hypocrisy? It may be found within the everyday expressions: sacredness and intellect; benevolence and morality; ingenuity and gain. None of these are inherent in humans but are artificially induced by reliance upon external influences. Therefore, however much we pursue them, not only will we not reach the ultimate truth as our true nature, but they will also become a source of distress and suffering. Moreover, they will give rise to selfishness, self-interest, and coldheartedness ultimately leading to disorder in society and even becoming a source of conflict. The history of humankind bears testimony to the above.

It is right now that we should awaken the true nature lying dormant inside us. This means casting off superficial appearance and endeavoring to reveal our real selves, looking at ourselves, by ourselves, anew. It also means returning to a heart of purity and simplicity as well as discovering sincerity and truth, and by doing so we will always be reflecting on our true nature. One's self-centeredness and selfishness should be recognized, and excessive feelings for others should be brushed aside to get rid of the ostentation surrounding one's true nature. Only the minimum amount of sufficient desire should be precisely selected while self-centeredness and greed should be rejected.

The heart and the stomach should always be kept empty in retaining a light body and mind while being thankful for the blessings of nature's beauty and human's kindness. Through devoting oneself to fulfilling one's given role and discovering the happiness in the fruits of one's efforts, the wonder of life may be experienced moment by moment, day by day. It is in returning to human's original simplicity that we find the significance of being in this world that comes from the Tao.

In the enterprise as well, it is vital to consistently return to its original social role and to exert all efforts in fulfilling the role of "improving society and life," but at the same time originality is also necessary. By looking at society in a unique way — "This company is like this" — the direction in which the company goes results in its individuality, and it is this that gives meaning to the company's existence in society. From society's side, a galaxy of able men and women and their various enterprises offer proposals to its many facets thus providing a richness of choices to customers. This indeed is the source of affluence.

What does "ambition" mean for us as humans? It is something indispensable, advancing society, and making the impossible possible. But it is also something difficult: if self-examination is neglected, there is no telling to what extent ambition will expand. Ambition is essential, but it is necessary to always reflect on oneself and discard ambition that is excessive.

Then, what exactly is "essential" ambition? It is ambition that promotes one's given roles and responsibilities, and the ambition rising within us should be so directed.

In order to promote "continuous fulfillment of development" in an enterprise, it is necessary to consistently provide values not existing elsewhere and this is where ambition and desire should be brought into play. The kind of ambition that an enterprise should have is one that is directed towards "always providing unique values as an attractive proposal for the betterment of society and life" and is given full play therein.

No. 20 I-ZOKU

From Confrontation
to Harmonious Coexistence

THERE IS A DISTINCT DIFFERENCE between the person who leads his or her life in accordance with the Tao and the modern kind of person who adheres to contemporary values. When we look at this carefully, the state of the follower of the Tao becomes clear.

Because many modern people look at things in relative terms, they inevitably make judgments based on comparisons. The slightest praise from others makes them feel on top of the world, while even a little criticism prompts despondence. When comparing themselves with others, if their positions are even slightly higher they feel as happy as if they had conquered the world, but when they are lower, they feel the sadness of someone who has fallen far from power. Further, when this kind of person tries to fulfill his or her own ambitions, she or he lives life busily searching for new opportunities, chasing even higher ambitions, and trying to become a canny, shrewd, and cunning person.

On the other hand, because the person who has deeply studied the Tao lives life according to the absolute and focuses intently upon unity with the Tao, she or he is never swayed by joy and sadness that come to seem superficial. All basics and all the secrets of proceeding through life harmoniously are sought from the Tao, asking and closely listening to the Tao. Efforts are made to acquire cosmic energy that in turn leads to a life of calmness and emptiness. At first glance, such a person may look quite different and even appear to be a simple rustic. Compared to the masses that live according to their own resources and their own intelligence, the person of the Tao lives his or her life with the aim of embracing the great source and being sustained by the Tao. When this happens, one's focus of attention will inevitably be directed not outside or towards others, but inside towards finding the Tao within oneself, towards self-control of one's inner ambitions, and towards inner composure.

For those at one with the Tao, there is no confrontation. Everything in this world and everything that happens at each moment is a result of the Tao, the great mother that gives birth to everything. Therefore, we who were born of the same mother are all siblings and properly there cannot be any conflict. Everything follows a fixed orbit throughout its life and eventually returns to the Tao. In a relationship where everything shares the same fate, can there be any confrontation? If there is conflict, it can be resolved by positively treating the factors that make the various opinions, different positions, and elements causing disagreement one and the same. Thus, there are no servile feelings associated with compromise and concession; it becomes a proper, very natural thing.

Creativity can overcome the obstacles and problems causing conflict. Overcoming in this sense does not mean causing the collapse or ruin of one party, rather it means accepting both parties and finding a third, transcendent arrangement or solution. If we carefully observe the world in

TAO Management

which we live, particularly the natural world, we discover many examples of two opposing parties in direct contradiction with each other who are living in peaceful coexistence. This is how the world was originally, but humans created conflict and contradiction as a result of their logical thinking. In other words, conflict and contradiction did not originally exist and are thus artificial.

Therefore, we must return to the original state of this world and recover ideas, ways of dealing with things, and even systems that transcend conflict and contradiction.

No. 21 KYO-SHIN

Great, Invisible Power

I HAVE BEEN TALKING ABOUT TOGETHERNESS AND UNITY with the Tao, but what precisely is this thing that we call the Tao? It is enchanting and difficult to grasp. What does this mean? Generally speaking, we do not accept, or recognize things that we cannot see. If we cannot accept things we cannot see, what about air? There can be no one who disputes its existence. There are also cases where something is so huge that all of it cannot be seen. Our way of thinking that denies existence to something simply because we cannot see it is clearly limited and needs to change. If we attain a certain state, some things that we normally cannot see become visible. What is this "certain state"? When we talk about seeing the Tao, it means maintaining tranquility and emptiness. One method of doing this is through meditation and if practice is carried out over many years, it is certainly possible to achieve a state of deep, near absolute tranquility and emptiness. If this condition is maintained even to a small extent, an image that can be likened to a cluster of light will emerge from the darkness. It feels as if one is meeting oneself, or more accurately, it seems like something from one's inner self. It is something indefinite: it can be said that it exists while it can also be said that it does not exist. However, there is no doubt that various things are actually felt. More certain and impressive than when we see something in front of our eyes, it is a sensation where we deeply feel the Cosmos itself.

Meditation, however, is not the only method. In normal life, there is sometimes the realization of being sustained or of the presence of a great, invisible power. It is precisely at these times when we feel the Tao.

Among people in the business world are those who are regarded as being of the same caliber as "world-class" athletes and gifted artists. Many of them possess a great and subtle power — let us call it cosmic energy — that combines the merits of both and is summoned and used at will, or in other words, they possess what seem to be extraordinary, even superhuman skills. When putting these exceptional skills into practice, there are common conditions. First, they put their whole body and soul into the work they are supposed to do and immerse themselves in the job completely. They are in a state of perfect selflessness. Next, they possess techniques — difficult to explain, difficult to express, and commonly known as know-how — that perfectly match the requirements of the situation at hand. When we look at how they match, it is through the summoning of cosmic energy in the most difficult of times. All these conditions are ones that are necessary for achieving unity with the Tao. Therefore, it should not be thought that unity with the Tao is exceedingly difficult. For people who are above a certain level, it is something that is always happening in their daily work.

The various methodologies making up Future Prediction, which is said to be the wisdom of ancient China, are based on the following way of thinking:

The atmosphere is made up of infinitesimal particles that are eight-cornered cubes. These particles are always oscillating at an amplitude of 340,000 millimicrons at longest, and 43 millimicrons at shortest, while we are able to see only from 76 millimicrons to 400 millimicrons and limited to seven colors. We can therefore see only a very small portion. An atmosphere with oscillation of more than 76 millimicrons is known as Taizokai (air of earth), while one of less than 400 milli-microns is called Kongokai (air of gold). The part visible to human eyes is called Jissokai, and comprises a very limited range of the atmosphere.

If this is to be believed, then there must be another un-fathomable, huge world on each side of ours. But the important thing is that, whether visible or not, the oscillation of the particles is carried out without regard to the boundaries of these worlds, and so the parts that cannot be seen nonetheless exert a great influence on our daily lives. Thus, the superiority and wonderful abilities of the world-class person who can see the invisible and hear what cannot be heard are not mysterious talents but rather, something that can be said to be in the natural heritage of humankind.

No. 22 EKI-KEN

Global-scale "Only One" Enterprise

WE ARE CREATED AND GIVEN LIFE BY THE TAO and eventually, turn around and return to the Tao. But what is the reason for us being put into this world? The answer is so that we remember our sense of unity with the Tao. Somehow, as soon as a human is born into this world, at that very moment, even the existence of the Tao is forgotten. After having had a tough struggle with something, we begin to notice the existence of the Tao and awaken to the eternal truth, but isn't this something we already possess when we are born? If so, clearly we should return to unity with the Tao as quickly as possible.

Why should we do this? Essentially, in order to complete the natural span of our lives. We should give serious and sustained consideration to the fact that, because great pains were taken to give us life in this world, we must fulfill our life spans. There is no joy in returning to the Tao in the middle of our lives when we should still be alive because of some sort of carelessness or mistake. Then what can we do to complete our life spans? The tree that is bent can complete its natural life because it is difficult to use and therefore spared from being cut down; the insect walks with its body curved so that it can walk straight; ground is indented so that it can hold water; and leaves wither and fall allowing new ones to grow. The less, the better. Few means easy to obtain; a lot means indecision and eventually gaining nothing. Thus the person who follows the Tao never tries to push himself or herself to the foreground and never rigidly sticks to her or his own ideas without yielding. Further, there is no boasting about one's own business achievements or one's abilities. On the contrary, there is always an attitude of humility and of keeping oneself in the background.

The person who attains this kind of mentality will be popular with others, win their trust, and receive their support in becoming a leader. There will never be conflict with others because the factors causing conflict will have been removed from oneself eliminating even the possibility of conflict. If there is no conflict throughout one's life, one's life will not be imperiled.

What is the reason for living in this manner? It is precisely because one places the greatest significance on completing life received from the Tao.

The reason why an Only One enterprise is desirable is because a company's duty lies in fulfilling its potential, which necessitates that management be safely, surely, and continuously conducted. It is far more important to focus all available energy on fulfilling the development of one's company rather than wasting it on such things as competition. Instead of competing, it is vital to have pride in the unique role of one's company, while being happy that it makes great contributions to society, and to fully devote oneself to one's work.

When we consider the energy consumed by competition, i.e., expended on advertising and sales as well as including the energy intake of supervisors and managers, it rapidly adds to a huge amount. Even on a global scale, providing or manufacturing certain products or services will be something unique from one's company and so, from all over the world, the people who desire them or to whom they are necessary, will be asking, "Sell it to me." Thus there will be absolutely no need to adopt the marketing stance of, "Buy it from me." Since there is no activity of selling as such, there is no sales department, no sales people, and therefore no selling costs. A particular product comes from one's company alone, and so there are no rivals and no competition, thus no competition cost. Resources saved are invested in reinforcing the "Uniqueness" of the company, on research and development expenses, and on recruiting and supporting superb development personnel.

The greatest hope that the Tao, the mother of everything, has for every person is that the life that has been sent out will return complete, in and of itself. To achieve this, contention with others should be replaced by the practice of humility. The Only One enterprise does not see worth in competition; it cultivates its unique social role and aims for its perfection.

No. 23 KYO-MU

Putting the Customer First, Oneself Second

THE TRUE CONDITION OF THIS WORLD is found in silence and tranquility. Typhoons that threaten to disrupt the world and torrential rains that can wash everything away do not last forever even though they are also actions of the almighty Tao. If this is the case, then it should be possible to sustain these tumultuous conditions for much longer. Why doesn't the Tao do this sort of thing? It is precisely because the condition of calmness is the natural condition of this world. Therefore, it is necessary for us to also live in accordance with this essence; the taciturn, quiet way of living is indeed natural. What do we mean by a quiet life? Basically, breathing is always regular, there is no fluster or astonishment, and the condition is maintained where breath is inhaled and exhaled from the abdomen. Blood should always be flowing from the head downwards and never the opposite, while sadness, fear, and anger are to be avoided. Because we are humans we do succumb to these kinds of emotions, but a return should be made to composure within a few moments.

It is important to adjust oneself to suit those that one is dealing with. The person of the Tao always tries to live in harmony with his or her opposites, whether they follow the Tao or not and whether they are people of virtue or without. When this happens, the other person will come to feel the joy of gaining a kindred spirit, the joy of gaining a friend. So, essentially, it becomes a case of giving happiness to others.

But what happens when the opposite occurs, when others are ignored and one's insistence on personal views is held constant? Not only will resistance and opposition be generated, but needless conflict will also be brought about. More than anything else, it is vital to remember that when we try to convey our opinions to the other party, if they do not listen to us then there is nothing we can do. It is important to get to know the people we deal with, be in tune with them, and establish lines of communication. If this does not happen, no matter how excellent our opinions are, they will not be heard and nothing will be achieved.

What should be our way of thinking to achieve the basis of this kind of living? It is, indeed, emptiness; and the essence of emptiness is truth. Making oneself empty does not mean having no opinions of one's own, having no principles of one's own, and certainly not being in tune with the other party merely to avoid conflict, which one dislikes. It means putting the other party first and oneself next. One's opinions should not be spoken first, but there should be an attitude of asking, "How about you?" The other's opinions should be heard first and from there points similar to one's own opinions should be found and responded to.

In the enterprise, importance should be placed on the customer above everything else. The customer is first, the company next. The company that adopts this kind of mentality is indeed a splendid one. All its ideas start from the viewpoint, "How is it for the customer?" Next the company asks what it can do to best realize these ideas. Then, because there are a wide variety of customers of different character and preferences, it should be the general rule to "adjust to the customer." What kind of character the customer possesses and what kinds of preferences he or she has should be verified and a shift should be made accordingly to provide the appropriate service. The worst thing that can happen is if there is some deception in the service — always hated by customers — that leads to the loss of customers. That is where there must be truth, but what is this truth? As an expert and professional, it is reliability and business ability; as a human, it is trust and sincerity.

No. 24 KU-ON

Eliminating Wasteful Excess

STANDING ON TIPTOE OR WALKING WITH LENGTHY STRIDES is behavior that cannot be long sustained. Instead, it becomes a hindrance because it is behavior that is unnatural. Then what is natural behavior? It is being in harmony with one's surroundings. It is not jutting forward, being prominent and conspicuous, nor any similar behavior.

One becomes a leader or someone noticeable very naturally when chosen by everybody in one's surroundings because they recognize one's achievements and abilities. Then, what does it mean to be recognized by those around us? It means always maintaining a consistent attitude with no double-dealing. There is no extreme change in one's behavior or utterances towards others. If there is double-dealing it means that there is contrivance merely to suit others, and even though there will be the illusion of having gained others' agreement, there will soon be resistance because it is not true agreement.

Whatever kind of action we undertake, rather than worrying about what others think and see, we should act in ways that convince and satisfy ourselves. In other words, it is a case of living for oneself by always looking within oneself for reference and direction. For someone leading life like this, judgment and recognition by others will be merely something extra. If priority is given to an external frame of reference and direction and one lives for its sake, then the purpose of life will not be understood. If you imagine that a person who makes himself or herself noticeable, boasts about his or her abilities and achievements, and thinks himself or herself to be the best is standing in front of you, how will you respond to that person? At the very least, you will probably think that it is not a person with whom you are willing to make efforts to become good friends. By having even a short conversation, doesn't it bring about feelings of opposition and competition within you? What if you have to sit next to each other for a long time? It will probably end up as a situation where you feel that you do not want to meet again. Not only will there not be acceptance, but there may also be a feeling of disownment or dismissal. Thus, from the viewpoint of the follower of the Tao, ignoring harmonious relationships with those around one precipitates disadvantages and becomes behavior that is wastefully excessive.

When we examine our lives, we can see just how much wasteful excess there is in our actions. The biggest is "excessive feeling" including such things as being overanxious. Harboring feelings of jealousy and suspicion towards others means achieving nothing constructive and results in complete waste. These kinds of useless emotions spread out in a ripple effect engulfing many people and eventually result in the waste of a gigantic amount of energy.

These feelings come from situations such as seeing things from a relative point of view. Oneself is oneself; it is not necessary to compare oneself with others. It must not be forgotten that we all have individual personalities, wonderful attributes which simply do not allow for comparison. In a situation where there is the potential of succumbing to useless emotions, we should relax, calmly close our eyes,

TAO Management

and while trying to maintain tranquility and emptiness, think about the fact that our great ally, the Tao, is with us.

So, in a business organization, along with eliminating work that is excessive, wasteful, and uneven, it is also very important to get rid of the useless emotions. In an enterprise it often happens that most employees spend the bulk of their energy on useless feelings. It is even said that these useless feelings are an inevitable adjunct of human organizations. Thus, eliminating wasteful energy results in dramatic changes that significantly improve the company's health.

The most effective way to carry this out is to have the directors themselves buckle down to the task of getting rid of their own useless feelings. The middle management should make everything clear and open, or make perfectly clear that which is not at the moment; that is, ensure fairness with everything aboveboard and try to remove any gray area that may lead to misjudgment, depending on the emotional state of a person who makes a decision in the company. Finally, inside the company itself, the employees must recognize the idea of an Only One enterprise and strive to promote it.

No. 25 SHO-GEN

Understanding the Cycle

WE SHOULD NEVER FORGET that we are the alter ego of the ruler of the great cosmos, the Tao. Therefore, it is wise to live in complete accordance with it. But how does it function? Everything that comes from the Tao is created by the Tao, goes away from it and eventually turns around, approaches, and finally returns to it; so it is the action of the Tao that expresses the movement of everything. It is exactly the same in the case of human life: we are created by the Tao, go away from it, turn around at some time in our lives and again, return. Death means returning to the Tao.

This also holds true for plants. The root sprouts buds that grow into a large tree that eventually dies as a return is made to the root. It also applies to things and events. Every event that happens or thing that appears, though they be great or small, will gradually return to a state of tranquility. It is the same for all creation. Thus, it is important that we thoroughly understand this Tao cycle.

TAO Management

Naturally, an enterprise reflects this cycle as well. After its establishment, growth continues and eventually there is a turnaround, maturity, then decline. It is the same for work, and the same for products. In the case of the enterprise, the period when the turn is made into maturity is especially important. This is because during the continuous period of growth after establishment, little is learned through its continued expansion. However, when maturity is achieved and pushing ahead with expansion slows dramatically, the pace becomes more relaxed, and many things can be learned. The combined knowledge and know-how from different kinds of experience would serve to facilitate the fresh establishment of a veteran company rich in experience. In corporate management, there can be no forgiving stagnation and decline, so that before business and products enter their period of maturity, a start must be made on the next business and products through utilizing the experience, know-how, and data acquired from the former, and constantly maintaining a parallel between the old/new business and products.

The cyclical action of the Tao also illustrates the great importance of centrifugal and centripetal forces. Initially, it is necessary for an enterprise to expand its scale of sales and service areas. Expansion for an enterprise means an increase in customers who recognize the company's worth; in other words, it means expanding its social role and thus is absolutely necessary. Ongoing expansion means enhancing the action of the centrifugal forces, which in turn means that the influence of the centripetal forces will gradually diminish. Thus, in the period of expansion, many measures that emphasize increasing the centripetal forces must also be utilized. It is essential that during this time, one trusts and is in alignment with the intentions of top management. From there will be born the pride of being a company member and the love for one's company. Therefore, how the top management personnel live and conduct themselves is of vital importance.

We say that humanity follows the earth. Without the earth humanity is impossible. This expresses our awareness that we live together with the earth, standing with both our feet firmly planted on it. We absorb all our nourishment and energy from the earth, and there is no wavering, no fluster, and no trouble.

The earth follows heaven, heaven follows the Tao, and that is exactly why the movements of the constellations in the sky are ordered and harmonized. This is why it is necessary to learn about this kind of action; it is this that is the action of the Tao.

To follow the Tao is to follow the way of nature. There is no intention in nature, no aim; it is a world that is unrestricted and limitless. How can we enter this domain of no limitation? Simply, to lead our lives by following the earth, heaven, the Tao, and if we live in this way, the limitless world will open before us. It is we who impose limits and the structures restricting freedom. Thus, it is vital to become one with the Tao and taste the possibility of non-limitation.

No. 26 JYU-TOKU

A Company of Composure and Firmness

IT IS SAID THAT HEAVINESS IS THE ROOT OF LIGHTNESS, and silence is the master of noise. While a person lives, to perform actions lightly with a nimble body is very important. An occasional flood of light music or the din of some noisy scene may prove to be indispensable stimuli for vigor and the powers of imagination. In corporate activity, it is necessary to answer customers' needs by using nimble footwork, thus accumulating social acceptance through their praise and applause. However, the more this kind of necessity, the more we should remember "firmness" and "calmness." Indeed, firmness and calmness should be deeply cultivated and strongly adhered to because they consolidate the basis of the company and thus make its actions possible.

The basic mainstay of the company, the management, should not forget this essential foundation. Firmness means always being careful not to stray from the most important points, in other words, not forgetting unity with the Tao, while calmness means continuing to maintain a viewpoint and attitude of composure.

There is nothing more important for human beings than the feeling of trust and its root is in the human character of firmness and composure. For top management, the most important factor is gaining the confidence of their personnel, clients, and business partners. It follows then, that there is nothing more important than to foster an attitude of firmness and composure that shapes the basic impression presented by top management as well as the other senior managers and supervisors. Rash and improper utterances should be avoided at all costs and so, just before acting or speaking, introspection is important.

For an enterprise as well, it is important to hold firmly to its main policies while calmly reflecting on the relationship between one's company and society, and rectifying that which needs correcting. Given this kind of corporate climate and this kind of backbone in the company, work can be carried out swiftly because of the nimble activities of those in charge at each workplace. Even if society praises and cheers hit products, it will be of insufficient influence to sway the company from its true form.

It is important to constantly maintain an attitude of "looking at the inside." For an enterprise, this means keenly observing how things are inside the company, the state of management, and the state of work. It means looking at things calmly and objectively, always being familiar with the various strengths and shortcomings, and whether there is an upturn or downturn in the present situation.

Outside the company, its reputation and what is said about it should be heard in the context of putting the present situation of the company and its capabilities first. It should not be forgotten that accurate response from the outside comes only after the company has established its true condition. Not being aware of this quickly causes the opposite result: precedence is given to judgment and impressions coming from the outside, from one's surroundings, and others, and in error, this comes to influence the development of one's company. When this happens, anxiety and instability occur as the outside influences determine every action and how to act becomes a matter of great concern and uncertainty. Eventually, confusion results and the company becomes like a puppet with the outside influences pulling the strings. The larger the organization the bigger the disturbance, and considerable time and energy is required for the situation to be neutralized, then stabilized.

From this point of view, it becomes clear how vital it is for the leaders to have the indispensable qualities of firmness and calmness. According to what one says and how one acts, one's sphere of influence changes. Thus, the higher one's position in the company or the bigger the company becomes, the more necessary it is to thoroughly anchor one's utterances and actions in these qualities. In other words, if leaders of big organizations do not thoroughly embrace firmness and calmness, the repercussions and losses will be immense.

No. 27 KOH-YOH

Into the Domain of the Master

WHEN WE TRY TO MAKE SOMETHING PROCEED as we ourselves want, it ends up without anything having been achieved because it is coercive and often, various kinds of damage will have been done. How can we set about creating a situation where things cannot help but proceed as we wish, a situation where many people cannot help but move toward the goal we want, and when such a situation is set and people start moving in this direction, we can just let the situation move on? We must first create a situation where no matter what route we take, we have to finally reach the goal. Next, we need to carefully "warm-up," get into the rhythm, and then apply this impetus to our actions.

When we look carefully at the work of a master, certain characteristics are apparent. For example, before branches are cut from a tree, its present condition is closely observed. Is it one of health? Is there abundant life? How are the branches and leaves growing? Next, harmony with the surroundings: are there overlapping branches or is there interference from neighboring trees? Then, the weather conditions and climate are closely observed: is a warm season or a cold season coming? In the process of cutting off the branches, will it rain or is the sun about to come out? Again the tree itself is looked at. If it is left as it is, which branches will grow in what way, and how will the overall balance be? After removing the branches, what kind of form should remain? The final form is vividly imagined as if it had already been finished. After this, from which branch to which branch is it best to carry out pruning? In other words, the most efficient and safest working process will naturally arise, and when this happens, it will also be clear as to where, against which branch, the ladder should be placed. From this, it will be understood what kind of saw with which kind of blade is necessary at what time and so thorough preparation can be made. If things can be visualized in this way, a relationship with the tree itself will have been created, and the tree will have a sense of security akin to trust in the fact that the most qualified person is coming to trim its branches. In other words, because an interrelationship is created between the tree and the person, work becomes very smooth, proceeds skillfully, and is completed with obvious competence, thus prompting requests for further work.

A master's work is truly natural, as easy as the blowing of the wind, and without the other party noticing, the master achieves his or her aims and departs with an air of nonchalance. She or he aligns smoothly with nature and becomes unified with it in carrying out his or her work.

To summarize the essential points: first, the other party must be carefully observed so as to recognize their likes and dislikes, habits and characteristics; however, the important thing is not to pass any kind of judgment about them. This means not comparing to one's own personal likes and dislikes, and not judging by comparing with other companies. It means simply to quietly get to know everything possible. If judgment is passed the other party will not be deeply observed from an objective standpoint.

Next, the overall flow should be read: social trends, the atmosphere of the company, the whole intention, etc. Then, the next thing to do is to invite the other party to ride with this current. In due course, they will have to give themselves wholeheartedly to its power. The other party must be understood, while a situation of affection and good relationship must be created. To achieve this kind of smooth work, understanding the complexity of human relationships is important. The Tao is not human in this way: it shows no prejudice towards anyone, it treats everyone the same, and it shows no favoritism. As the Tao does not see relatively, so there is no comparing, nor does it harbor prejudice towards humans. It never sees by comparing strengths and abilities; rather, it looks at individual character and distinctive qualities.

If these special qualities of the Tao are learned, all personnel will be treated in the same way and will come to work diligently by applying their individual skills. If all employees share the same abilities, skills, and temperament, no one will be able to deal with those problems that arise outside their areas of competency. If company personnel are comprised of people with wide ranging skills and abilities, the most suitable job can be chosen for each particular person. Thus, whatever kind of problem occurs, there will always be someone qualified to take care of it. This is what makes an organization truly strong. The essential point is matching the allocation of the work necessary with the appropriate person, thus facilitating bringing out the best in each staff member.

No. 28 HAN-BOKU

Internalizing Outside Resources

STRENGTH IS NECESSARY FOR HUMANS and it also has the characteristic of being fragile. While being aware of this complementary quality of strength, it is important to maintain awareness of those things that form the complete opposites of strength, namely, weakness and softness as well. When this is done, the relative elements of strength and weakness, firmness and softness will become unified in perfect harmony and the resulting fullness and depth of complete strength that transcends complementarity will make it possible to deal calmly with everything in one's world. Living will become very natural and without strain upon one's system, so all things will proceed smoothly.

Things of purity are necessary. However, that which can easily become dirty as well as that which is dangerous should be known. While being aware of the quality of purity, one enters into the midst of turbidity, thus "mingling with the common world." In other words, both knowing about the pure heart and also putting oneself into the whirlpool of ambition in the street are important. This means that one needs extensive and balanced knowledge of the qualities and elements that make up this world without being at a loss as to how to deal with them. At times a sense of luxury is also necessary, but its accompanying evils of hollowness as well as the grudges and jealousy of others should not be forgotten.

Further, for someone who endeavors to lead a life of humility, such an attitude will earn genuine trust from others and will result in many people's recommendation for leadership. As this kind of leader, the other's various qualities should be learned, and without expressing preference for either, both sides should be understood when being relativistic. When an attitude of humility is maintained, a situation of "everything can be seen" will arise. The multitude of inconsistencies inherent in each person and all the various feelings and emotions in organizations such as an enterprise will be understood. The relative parties — the individual, the group, the organization — will come to be clearly visible from the inside to the outside, and from the surface to the inner depths. Having this kind of knowledge in one's dealings will thus lead to smooth progress in everything one does.

In the enterprise, developing a leader's capabilities in how to best utilize human resources, or "putting the right person in the right place," is important, and one key measure of management is whether placement of personnel with the correct abilities and characters for their roles is carried out. If we consider that it is common nowadays to recruit personnel from the outside, then to what degree and extent they are trusted and used as one's own employees becomes very important and the scope of the leader's delegation of "right people in the right place" rapidly expands. Given the importance of this kind of ability, it is vital that "everything can be seen" by the one who leads.

But is it possible for a person of simplicity to have insight into one who is complicated? Is it possible to grasp the various factors of a problem in their entirety for one whose character shows partiality? It is possible if one can have more complicated and more varied elements within oneself than the personnel or problems targeted.

What exactly comprises the trust that subordinates have in their leaders? It is in knowing that no matter how strong the other party is or whether a request is simple and plain or something complex and splendid, the leader has the ability to maintain a constant attitude and solve each problem as it arises. Simply, it shows as a sense of security in knowing that the leader possesses unmatched abilities.

Respect for the ability to bring out the skills of the organization as a whole is another component. From the point of view of the employees, if they continue intently to fulfill their given roles then they will achieve the aims of the company. This will mean that all members of the organization will have achieved their aims and there will be a strong synergy at work in the whole of the company. In other words, all personnel of the organization will have admiration for the abilities of the general leader who can make the whole company work well and will therefore trust him or her.

From the leader's point of view, it is necessary to create the situation of "everything can be seen" and to maintain the ability of being able to do this. Subordinates' trust will not be gained from simply respecting their character; conversely, neither will it be forthcoming to one who simply fights or whose only ability is one of tact. The leader should be a person of a deeply varied and complex nature although one who normally does not show it, but rather gives the appearance of a rural scholar with the air of a good-natured person. This indeed is the kind of model for the leader to aim for.

No. 29 MU-I

The World Moves as the Tao Wills
— So Does the Company

THE WORLD MOVES AS THE TAO WILLS. It has an independent will of its own and so moves beyond human control.

So does the company. Therefore, the more one wants to make it one's private property the more the result will be alienation. The more emphasis is placed upon private ownership, the more difficult it is to control the reins, and the person who gets too attached can eventually lose the company. Even for a company created from scratch, when a certain scale has been reached, the number of employees has increased, and the number of clients has grown, it does not mean that the founder can act capriciously or willfully. Even if one tries it is not possible; there will be some kind of resistance causing obstruction. In the case of strong resistance, even the founder can be driven out. This is because there is always the presence of the enterprise's life within an enterprise that functions like an individual will. What does this mean?

Everything in this world is a creation of the Tao. Therefore, the nature of everything is the nature of the Tao. The action of opposition to the Tao will, even if carried out, not proceed smoothly. If one persists, the result will end up being completely opposite. All humanity is a part of the Tao as are all companies. Therefore, if one part of something selfishly tries to move another part of the same thing according to its own convenience and self-interest, there will be a strain on the thing itself; action running counter to the Tao. Acting because of self-interest tends to breed disregard for the processes of nature that in turn tends to be action violating the Tao. All efforts are made to forcibly attain one's aims and the result is a resistance to the flow of nature's energy. When this happens, the more one wants to achieve strength the weaker things will become, while conversely, going for weakness means greater strength will result. The more one wants to raise one's achievements, the more they will decline; the more effort there is to reduce deficits, the more they will increase.

We must be fully aware that the company has already begun to exist individually with its own will. Next, which direction this will is flowing and how and what it aspires to must be carefully ascertained. Then, in the midst of this flow, opportunities must be found for the company to proceed as one intends and the endeavor must constantly be made to foster them. Carrying out actions coercively, artificially, or through one's exaggerated strengths should be avoided at all costs.

If the management's intention is not something artificial to satisfy self-interest but proceeds in the direction of constant fulfillment of the company's potential — the direction of the natural flow of the company — it will mean effective application of natural energy thus making for smooth progress. What can be drawn from this is that a manager is someone whose role is to grasp the will of the company, steer the company towards the direction of how it should be, and let it ride its natural flow. In the case of a ship, it means being the ship's captain, not the ship's owner. To go further, it means being a meteorologist, not making the weather. Thus, there must be no self-exaggeration. For example, if the meteorologist tries to exceed his or her function by attempting to influence the weather itself, he or she will be ruined.

However, this is a surprisingly common occurrence in the world of management. The manager sees her or his position as the pinnacle and adopts an air of arrogance. Or else, when indulging in a life of luxury, it leads to a false understanding of her or his role and position. From the perspective of the flow of natural energy, such a selfish person acts in an unnatural way resulting in a short life and expulsion from the company itself.

It must never be forgotten that both the company and oneself are parts of the Tao.

No. 30 KEN-BU

Forming a Noncompetitive Market

ACCOMPLISHING DESIRES through the use of force, and using military power to become stronger was what Lao-tzu hated most about war. It meant the coercion and subjugation of people by force, especially problematic because neither these kinds of actions nor that kind of energy flow are natural. It is poles apart from the Tao and is a flow not found in the Tao, so at first, damage is done to oneself. Then, because it evokes resentment and hatred from the other party, even winning means eventual retribution.

What exactly is this thing we call "living"? It means forming the basis of what is necessary to live, creating and making food, clothing, and shelter by oneself. Basically, every day, one's own efforts and own labor are used to produce food. Presently it is something mainly done by specialists, but the basics do not change.

War and the use of military force means plundering the fruits of the efforts and labors of others, or else trampling them under foot. This runs counter to the smooth flow of nature manifest as the flow of worldly energy, and therefore a reaction will always occur. Thus, this kind of action is completely futile. Powerful military force itself changes people's consciousness and ways of thinking, while power creates arrogance and loss of humanity and leads to pursuit of further power. The arrogance arising from power belittles others and often leads to a desire to employ military force. But as the faculties of military force and the armed forces are but one subsidiary element among many, the concept of making them uniquely powerful is in itself unnatural.

Concentrating on less forceful and nonmilitary elements should be encouraged because prompt action for avoiding political, economic, and diplomatic war will be called for. Even if a war has been won, since whether one has won or lost is only one result amongst many, boasting about winning has no meaning, while the action of following up one's victory and attacking further is an immoral act, a futile action to be abhorred.

Robustness is an omen of decline. Immorality is an omen of ruin. As rigorous physical labor requires the constant use of one's full energy and is a situation of strain, not only can it not continue forever, but it will also quickly become exhausted and spur decline. Immorality means going against the natural flow of worldly energy like trying to proceed up river against swift currents, and not only is it something that cannot continue but also something that leads quickly to destruction and ruin.

It is the same in an enterprise. The company must realize that competing is unnatural and promptly become an Only One company producing unique products, and form a competition-free market. Because the only company producing a particular product will be one's own, there will be no need to spend energy on competition, while the funds otherwise committed to the cost of competition can be invested in improving the product and reinforcing the concept of an Only One enterprise. Further, the product of one's company solely creates a market for one's company's product. It becomes a market that has not had prior exis-

TAO Management

tence and therefore creates a new situation and new opportunities for the maker and buyer to meet. This indeed is the fundamental aim of business.

The competition-free product and the Only One enterprise are the fruits of human wisdom and creativity and as such are among the greatest expressions and creations of humanity. In a company where this kind of true humanity is at work, happiness in creation will in turn stimulate further creation. Noncompetition results in an absence of physical and mental fatigue where energy is always in abundance and in reserve, bringing about flexibility — the most essential element for an organization — in the enterprise.

If robustness is the omen of decline, then flexibility is the omen of ongoing fulfillment of the company's potential. For the company with no competitive goals, it should be considered an indispensable element for its development.

No. 31 EN-BU

In Pursuit of Freedom

EXCELLENT WEAPONS are tools that bode ill for all. Why is this? What is the ultimate thing that we should be seeking? Is it prosperity? Fame? Success? Power? Influenced by other people's opinions and the abundance of available goods, there is no end to our desires and however much we obtain will not be enough. Rather, what we should be seeking is something within ourselves. The various ways that we achieve satisfaction, e.g., experiencing being happy, thankful, or excited, are easily changeable and unreliable. Thus, what we should be pursuing is that which is opposed by nothing, freedom. It is a situation where when we are attached to nothing, nothing remains in our hearts. There is no worry, no anxiety, no anger, no fear, and no sadness, the reason being that there is no source that gave them birth. What is their source? The answer is self-interest, wherein we try to do something dictated by our desires, and because of this, artificiality and coercion are created. It also causes us to try to exclude those who oppose our thinking. The result is battle; competition is caused and there is a need for excellent weapons. The opposite is also true. Excellent weapons cause conflict, ways of thinking, and self-interest that result in forming attachment. In other words, considered from the perspective of what humanity ultimately seeks, freedom, they are factors of ill-boding causing retrogression. As there are a great number of people in this world who epitomize the personification of self-interest, even if we do not desire to do battle it will often come to us.

What is the best thing to do in such cases? Everything in this world comes from the Tao, so that which is not in accordance with the Tao lacks smoothness, becomes overstrained, and suffers ruin. Putting it another way, if one obeys, follows, and lives in accordance with the Tao, there will be little chance of being entangled in conflict or being provoked. Even if it does happen, we will be given methods to avoid conflict enabling us to devise the most appropriate countermeasures. What should be done in the situation where there is no other recourse than to fight? When it cannot be helped, weapons should be used sparingly and unnecessary attacks should be avoided. When victory has been achieved hostilities should immediately be halted, without follow-up battles to satisfy mercenary desires or personal grudges. Nor should there be acceptance that war is a good thing in the first place.

It is the same for corporate activity. The aim should be to sell Only One products in a competition-free market, but there are also situations where conflict cannot be avoided. In such cases the most important factor is the leader's composure. The leader must exercise self-control and never become hotheaded. If conflict becomes the aim itself, it will be the worst kind of situation where the reason for fighting will have been forgotten.

Because the instinct to fight is inherent in humans and because a human is an animal that likes fighting itself, he or she will inevitably seek the agreeable feeling of confrontation, and will become absorbed in it when striving for victory. Remember that conflict is a thing to be avoided in the first place. Then to what should we apply our fighting spirit? Not to fight with others but to fight with oneself. There are an infinite number of problems and themes with which to do battle: perfecting one's own special abilities; improving one's professionalism; high achievement as a human group; and development of group creativity as an organization. It is to these and others similar that our inherent fighting spirit should be passionately directed.

TAO Management

No. 32 SEI-TOKU

What Is a Superior Manager?

THE TAO IS A HARMONIOUS COMBINATION of a surprisingly vast variety of diverse elements. Therefore, for want of a better name, it was called the Tao or "The Way." I have just called them "diverse elements" meaning that they originate from the Tao and eventually become independent and individual things. It is fair to call such elements diverse, but when inside the Tao they are in a unity that defies using this term. Putting it strongly, it is a situation of chaos. Putting it still another way, it is Araki. Just cut from trees in the mountains, Araki is rough timber, unaltered in any way. If we consider that eventually a multitude of diverse products will be produced from this timber, then it can be said that there is a harmonious unity of diverse elements. This unity of diversity can be said to be the source of possibility in this world as well as the source of creativity. However, the original form has no desire for decoration or show; it is simple and profound.

To begin following the Tao or making the Tao one's model, it must be studied as this kind of fertile chaos, the source of possibility, and as something simple and profound. No matter how low the position, the person who deeply studies and follows the Tao will have an aura of leadership and rule about him or her, that may prompt the reluctance of others to consider such a one as subordinate. Moreover, for one in a high position of leadership in an enterprise, unity with the Tao will be put into even more play. Because there are diverse elements within, one will have clear insight into various employees' natures and qualities, assign the right person to the right place, and make personnel happy by allowing them to fulfill their roles. She or he will be able to perceive the nature of any kind of occurrence and be able to deal with it appropriately which will result in everything proceeding in a smooth and very natural way.

As a manager of an enterprise, this kind of person is capable of becoming highly effective and justly famed worldwide. The ultimate goal of an organization led by this kind of noted manager is to be a company that does not need rules. The points of caution established by the regulations of the usual company will have already been accepted by all personnel as being matters of fact. Nor will there be the need to issue instructions and orders one by one. Employees will themselves be aware of what their roles entail and will act on their own judgment in the spirit of professional businesspeople, while new ideas will be frequently proposed to the management.

What is the basic need of the manager who will foster this kind of company? Indeed, it is being in accord with the Tao, but what does this mean? The chaos of diverse elements in harmonious union is the Tao, and from there, the diverse elements are then brought forth as independent and individual elements and are given names to distinguish them from each other. Doing this means bringing about relative opposition, distinction, and discrimination and is called "Logos," logical understanding or intellectual perception. In other words, following the Tao means having grasped the unity of various elements such as absolute understanding and insight through one's direct experience while dealing with each thing intellectually, one by one. Because of this, each element that has transcended the whole can be understood and as well as knowing the limitations and relativity of individual elements, it will be possible to apply them making full use of their qualities. As a result, each element, in the company each employee, and each operation in the company comes together as a small stream that forms a great river, and eventually, like the great river flowing into the sea, all the actions of all employees return to the manager. Still further, because the whole operation — the result of the whole organization — becomes clearer, those who participate in and are connected with the work will respect the manager and will give their willing cooperation. This is like seeing the process of everything arising from the Tao and eventually returning to it.

No. 33 BEN-TOKU

All Answers Are within Oneself

WE WORRY TOO MUCH about and show too much interest in our surroundings. When we look at people's lifestyles or their family troubles, we feel uncomfortable when others are a little happier than ourselves while we may want to intervene in situations less fortunate than our own.

It is the same in an enterprise, as great interest seems to be shown in the details of other companies engaged in the same kind of business. Because this kind of condition exists, there is a growing trend of respecting those who have been deemed "people of wisdom" because of their knowledge of other industries, companies, societies, and countries. Only being concerned with the outside leads to the absurd situation of losing trust in oneself and having greater confidence in the above kind of person than in oneself.

All answers are inside one's self. Looking at oneself, revealing oneself — this indeed is looking at the Tao, revealing the Tao. This is the way to achieve true wisdom. Trying to compete with and conquer others is futile because it eventually leads to loss of self-control, damage to health, and a shortening of one's life. It is oneself, not others, who should be conquered. Thus, the truly wise are those who have conquered themselves.

In an enterprise too, instead of comparison only with other companies, importance should be placed on achieving absolute personal satisfaction. Rather than using others' opinions as a standard without being satisfied — even though the opinions may be true — it is important to have an attitude of pursuing true personal satisfaction. The importance of this can be seen if we look at the history of technological innovations to date or products that have contributed to society's development: the companies that broke through the barriers of business "common sense" became top enterprises in the following years. Going against accepted business sense means understanding "unacceptable" business sense through utilizing one's company's particular values, something other companies were unable to do. Thus, above everything else, there must be a high degree of personal satisfaction through which we can also understand the meaning of true wealth.

Is there such a thing as a standard of being wealthy? If we look at the quantity of one's assets as a standard, if the owner has not hitherto achieved satisfaction then one can hardly be called wealthy. Again, looking to the outside is futile and it teaches us that not sheer quantity of assets but personal satisfaction is the indispensable factor. When full satisfaction is felt, it cannot be said that the person is wealthy at that very moment. Nor can it be said that the person has achieved success in life. The person who is truly successful is one who has been able to control his or her heart and mind, one who has overcome self-interest and personal feeling and, as a result, has found a state of freedom; or, it is someone who has begun to take steps in this direction.

When we become engrossed in conquering ourselves, the continuous effort, enthusiasm, and the feeling of satisfaction are already the very things that will have uncovered the meaning of life and what it really is that we should always be making an effort to seek in our lives. Indeed, it is this that expresses the meaning of the will to improve the present situation, and spending each and every day this way, or becoming like this, will allow us to realize the significance of why we were born into this world. It is the person who spends her or his life in this way that deserves to be called someone who has a truly long life, not the person who has simply piled up the years.

It is the same for a company that has no goals in the usual sense. The real purpose should be to create motivation by overcoming the company's deficiencies and weak points as a human group, and making a full effort to achieve perfection step by step — this is the direction of the ultimate enterprise.

TAO Management

No. 34 NIN-SEI

Who Owns the Company?

JUST LIKE WATER, the Tao flows in all directions. Like water, it can effortlessly permeate into any opening and simply spreads naturally. This happens because, though being the parent of all existence, the Tao does not make any attempt to broadcast this fact. Neither does it boast about its skills even though it has created so much, nor does it claim ownership of things because of having created them. This is why everything obeys the Tao, has admiration for it, and tries to return to it. Therefore, it is why everything proceeds to follow the cycle of first obediently expanding and then eventually turning around and returning to the Tao. From where does this condition of the Tao arise? It is from being without desire, without intention, as if its purpose is in the very act of carrying out the cycle itself.

In the enterprise as well, just like water, the aim is to spread one's company's products all over the world, though it must begin naturally. What can be learned about natural flow from the permeation of water is that water itself does not have any inclination to push itself ever forward. If the topography is low, the water flows by utilizing this topography

— the form of the other party. The more it continues to flow, the more vigorous it becomes, and when this happens even small obstacles will be washed away. Water can penetrate into the smallest of openings and has the flexibility to adapt its flow to any shape or form. Because its aim is to continue flowing, it does not make claims about itself nor does it try to get involved in useless argument.

From the beginning, the flow of products must be natural, which means not being disseminated through the power of the seller but flowing because of the power of the buyer. The product must be attractive for the buying public; it must be something that can make people say, "I've been waiting for this." Or there must be a situation where, like a surge of waves, customers who first purchase and use the product are completely taken by it and attract further customers. A true product must be something that is both necessary and attractive for the customer as well as being something that is made and popularized in conjunction with the customer. So, the enterprise is, in fact, a three-party alliance of managers, employees, and customers. The managers and the employees may have produced the goods, but this was done only because of the existence of the customer so to go into detail about the efforts and contributions of each that went into making it will be unnecessary. Even if the product becomes an unprecedented hit on a global scale it is because of the power of the customer and so there should not be any pride in one's own contributions. When a hit product is created, corporate achievements rise and the company develops. However, because it is a joint operation with society and mainly the customer, there should be no singing the company's praises, but rather an ongoing endeavor to be strong behind the scenes while silently preparing for further duties.

Is there any danger for a company that provides indispensable products for a huge number of people, always acting modestly, always striving to illuminate a certain nook of society by its honesty of putting quality first, and because of this, has a wide range of regular customers always supporting the company? The great joy when a product becomes even a slight hit is typically accompanied by an attitude of treating customers high-handedly, while managers being managers, there is pride in the company's business and pride in its expansion, which finally leads to treating the company as nothing but one's private property. Considering the preponderance of such examples, it is clearly important for the company to advocate the Tao.

No. 35 JIN-TOKU

The Essence Is Tranquility and Dignity

NO MATTER HOW MUCH WE TRY to talk about the importance of living in accordance with the Tao, we cannot explain everything in words, and our explanations become vague when we attempt to do so. The Tao itself cannot be pointed out or shown and is thus something with little power of persuasion. But can the existence of the Tao be explained logically? There are things in this world that cannot be seen but that truly exist in essence. They cannot be seen precisely because of this kind of existence, and because they greatly transcend our powers of thinking. However, we are able to feel their vastness and their power.

The person who follows the Tao, who takes the Tao as her or his model for living, can live a quiet and peaceful life without being threatened by misfortune or harm wherever one may be. But why should this be so? Simply, as everything in this world was created by the Tao with the same qualities and nature, thus all things exist in a symbiotic relationship.

The Tao has no self-interest, nor does it expect anything. This is why it dislikes selfish thought and action, and as long as the endeavor made to protect this symbiotic relationship is ongoing, there will never be any separation from this source that is the Tao. The Tao becomes us; we become the Tao. Those who are the Tao will never meet with calamity.

From the position of being at one with the Tao there is no need to call out in a loud voice, no need to attract attention. It is something very ordinary. The Tao is simple and pure, not some decorative element that wants to show itself to others. The ultimate purpose of life is to eliminate useless feelings and actions and to become a person who is like a child. The more we try to talk about the true nature of the Tao, the more unsuitable and inaccurate are high-sounding descriptions and the claptrap of overexaggeration. Speaking about the Tao thus becomes something done in an extremely simple way. Everyone is interested in and swayed by such attractive things as fantastic entertainment and fine music, but the true nature of the Tao is essentially an ordinary, everyday thing for us and so few people are as interested in it.

This is the character of the Tao and thus the true nature of human society can be found in tranquility and dignity. It is not something busily rushing around enforcing its will, but rather it is where the fundamental elements of peace and stability in human society can be found.

However, society seems to be careening along in a completely different direction. Looking back with nostalgia on the tranquility and dignity of even ten years ago, the difference is clearly visible. Thus, we should not fall under any spells or be misguided by anyone but should always continue to maintain tranquility and dignity in our hearts.

In the case of corporate management as well, tranquility and dignity are all too often lost in corporate activities. What can be done to retain this true nature? Strict adherence to the basic principles:

As an Only One enterprise, always putting the customer first by continuously using one's special corporate strengths to offer unique, high-value goods and services.

Recognizing the company as the perfect place to allow its employees to spend their working lives with the motivation of raising their abilities and achieving their goals.

 **No. 36 BI-MEI**

Weakness Is Superior to Strength

WHEN THE WORLD, and thus the action of the Tao, tries to reduce anything, without exception it first expands it. In the same way, if something is to be made weaker, there is strengthening at first; if stronger, then weakening occurs first. It is the same in recovery from an illness where before getting better, one gets worse. This is repeated. The relevant question here is in which direction, generally, are things proceeding? While both are repeated, are things gradually heading towards a complete recovery, or getting worse? Are progress and regression in the raising of ability or in acquisition of a skill repeated? Simply, is there a general flow of improvement or otherwise?

The combination of these two things that are alternating is very delicate but the effect is striking. What is the basis of this principle? It is that the same thing does not continue for long. If we look across a period of several days, there are ones on which the wind is strong while there are also days when there is no wind at all. When we look at the days of strong wind, strong gusts of wind alternate with moments when there is no wind. Thus, when we talk about wind, it does not mean that the wind continues to blow with the same constant unchanging strength.

The action of the Tao is multifarious and so it continues to give birth to an infinite number of diverse things. The same goes for cosmic energy; it is not expended or released constantly or without change.

In corporate activity as well, the key is whether good use is made of these two reciprocal elements; i.e., in what way activity and rest, dispersion and collection, expansion and reduction are controlled. Management is all about whether arrangement and implementation of these elements can be carried out effectively. Hence, planning is crucial, and it is in the expression of planning and strategic skills that the beauty of management appears when dealing with others.

If we consider strength and weakness, they are the same thing coming from the Tao. Therefore, identical elements are inherent within them.

Strength is something that also has a weakness or an Achilles heel. When weakness is changed into flexibility, it immediately has strength. The secret is to transcend each as well as treat both as being identical. When this is done, sometimes weakness is necessary and sometimes strength is necessary and so the division between strong and weak points, good and bad points will disappear. Thus, weakness also becomes something indispensable and whether it is effectively utilized becomes important. From this basis, the idea of "flexibility is superior to strength" can be readily understood and if we realize that strength and weakness can be identical, we need only flexibility to make good use of each.

Absolute power, superior weapons, and the power and ability that form strength cannot be treated simply and carelessly nor should they be brandished about lightly or on a whim.

In the company, the full power and authority of personnel management should not be wielded lightly or recklessly because the person on the receiving end has no power of opposition. When the other party is weaker than oneself and has no power of resistance, absolute power must not be exercised; it is behavior unbecoming of a human being. Issuing orders from a position of strength creates a one-sided relationship which means that there is a lack of harmony, which in turn inevitably leads to trouble. Similarly, not revealing one's weapons means displaying one's strength, while the more one's best weapons are put to use the weaker their effect becomes and the more one employs one's absolute powers the more effectiveness is lost. This implies that there are no absolute powers to be exerted for a final solution. Therefore, if one employs one's own powers too readily, it may not settle the situation, but rather cause trouble or even precipitate one's downfall.

The company's real strength, i.e., capabilities or technologies superior to its rivals, should not be shown off easily or heavily relied upon, but be carefully treated and further strengthened for real needs.

No. 37 I-SEI

The Enterprise Useful to Society Will Prosper

WHAT SHOULD WE TREAT as being more important than anything else? Let us seek for the answer in the Tao. In spite of the fact that the Tao is without purpose and intent, it does not mean that nothing is achieved. More than that, it is because of nonaction that things are achieved. What is the meaning of this? When we become deeply engrossed in something, does it mean that there is purpose and intent? Or, when we try to overcome some irrational danger that is staring us in the face, is there any intent in the extraordinary strength that is produced within us? Basically, we can say that when there is no need to bring our own logic and selfish arguments into things, or when there is no time to do this, it becomes a situation of nonaction. When we struggle with something and become completely engrossed or devoted to it, that is a situation of nonaction, and it is this kind of engagement in which our abilities and energy bloom and are most brought into play. Therefore, becoming absorbed, the exercise of concentration, and other such activities must be practiced.

To enter this kind of situation naturally and without strain a certain amount of technical skill is necessary. The standard level of skills must be mastered first. But it is no good if the process of mastering such skills gives you only pain but no joy. Thus, it is something that has to be done on the premise of "liking it." This means finding something that we do because we like doing it, and this indeed is what education is. It means being given the chance to try all sorts of things and while doing something, it will become clear whether one has the aptitude for it or whether it is suitable. Thus, "finding something one likes" is important in our lives, and it is a good thing there are many such educational opportunities.

Doing through nonaction means having work where one almost forgets oneself in one's devotion, and because one is doing something one likes, there is no feeling of tiredness even after several hours. Liking what one does leads to rapid proficiency. However, if things are carried out simply for one's own satisfaction this kind of rhythm will become sluggish and eventually come to a stop.

So, what lubricates the wheels of this motion? Feedback or reactions from society and the judgment of customers provide the indispensable element of "contributing to society." We are not born alone, brought up alone, nor do we go through our lives alone; we live in partnership with a great number of people. What becomes vitally important is our relationship with others, our relationship with society.

To put it another way, the richness of life is first felt after having established a relationship with others and society, and, further still, it can be said that this is exactly the reason why we were born. We meet with a great number of people, naturally interact, and life is where the different kinds of stories that are created from these experiences allow us to truly feel the blessings of being alive.

Therefore, above all, what we give back to others and society is very important. "Giving back" does not mean only on the large scale of tangible contributions, it also means how we respond. With a smile? To make others comfortable? We have to start from here.

Within nonaction is included the criticism of "placing too much emphasis on broad knowledge." Such a person is caught in the trap of fashionable logic or of showy but shallow ideas and culture. Engagement with nonaction instead directs one's attention to the original condition of a human-to-be and encourages one to attend to its pursuit.

If intention and purpose are completely removed, what can possibly be left? It is the pure-heartedness, the sincerity found within us. Humans as well as corporations should return to this state and look at it anew: What is sincere living? What is culture? What is corporate activity? What is customer service?

No. 38 RON-TOKU

Basic Principles of Humans and Management

THE TRUE PERSON OF VIRTUE is not conscious of this condition, but one's action is that of the Tao. If done consciously it cannot be said that virtue is being practiced. When practiced unconsciously, it seems to exude from the whole body and the sincerity of what is said and done can be clearly understood, which encourages the other party to reciprocate in the same way. The more people in top positions of society and organizations become like this, the more will those under them be influenced and, therefore, the better society and organizations will be.

When virtue is superficial and done solely for the sake of appearance or formality, not only does it cease to be called virtue, but also it is inevitable that society and all organizations will follow suit. It is not something that is gradually formed and then penetrates into the body. Thus, the leeway of "waiting" becomes important and for society and organizations it is this "waiting" that becomes the basis of bringing up people.

The enterprise knows no end. Through "continuous development of fullness" its premise is one of eternal continuance that suggests a long-term policy of personnel development be adopted. There is a common tendency to focus upon developing personnel who will immediately become useful, but instead of technical training for an outward appearance of efficiency or inhumanly excessive mental training, it is necessary to give training in the basic principles of being human in order to develop leaders who will form the basis for the company's immortality. It is different if one wants a short-lived company, but if there is an aim for permanency and a wish for continuance, then there is no other remedy except to implement "waiting" training.

For this, a "twenty-year personnel training plan" is necessary; twenty years to polish up on basics. More than anything else, a firm foundation must be laid, and this foundation is: Basic human principles and basic principles of management.

Basic human principles are formed from three elements.

First, grasping the philosophy of the Cosmos. Humans as well as society exist within the Cosmos and it is essential to comprehend its laws. Things that are human-made occupy only the tiniest part of the vast, boundless Cosmos. Because everything obeys its laws, to attempt those things that run contrary to these laws will not achieve success. Therefore, understanding the philosophy of the Cosmos forms the basis of being human.

Second, learning correct human behavior. Without knowing what behavior is correct or not, one cannot be sure how to begin and then continue one's work. So, one should learn how to act or behave as if the philosophy of the Cosmos has become embodied in human deeds.

Third, grasping the significance of life. The significance of a human being is what one achieves throughout the course of one's entire life. To make one's life significant, the correct behavior and actions one learns and has learned must be implemented and exercised meanwhile proceeding to climb the stairway of life day by day, step by step. A method that prevents running out of breath, such as making continuous learning the habit of one's lifetime, is helpful. There is an old saying that simplifies these basic human principles as follows:

Learning in youth becomes useful in the prime of life.
Learning in the prime of life means strength in old age.
Learning in old age means no decay even after death.

How can these three elements be learned? The Chinese classics, which explain the abstruse mechanism of these theories with simple and clear words, are an excellent resource for further study.

No. 39 HOU-HON

Giving Attention to Harmony — The Cosmic Law

THE TAO CONSISTS OF TWO OPPOSING FORCES or complements, i.e., long and short, simple and difficult. Because there is shortness, there is length. Because there is difficulty, there is simplicity.

It is the same with success and failure, nobility and humility, and it is because there is the element of failure that there is success, which means that because there is someone lowly, there is someone noble. This is balance and harmony; there is no possibility of one-sidedness because there is a return of energy to the opposite side. The secret of being successful, or noble, is to constantly maintain this balance because of "gaining and losing." If only the situation of "gaining" is continued then "losing" will occur to rectify the balance and there will be loss in oneself. Thus, the approaches of "donation and volunteer" or "modesty and humility" should be cultivated along with "gaining." It is essential to maintain an awareness of the state opposite of what one is. One can be successful when there is someone who is not, and the person of nobility can be so because of the lowly person. On a more personal level, one should maintain balance oneself by continuously embracing an attitude of modesty and humility. The simplicity and naïveté so much liked by Lao-tzu is of this order.

In corporate management, departments to promote success such as a Management Planning Department and a Business Promotion Department have been the norm, but from now on, it will become important to have a department for maintaining balance. Let us call it the "Harmony Promotion Department" for the moment. The function of this department consists of two parts: Harmony with Society and Harmony in the Company.

1. Harmony with Society

Objective data should be collected on the situation of the company in society as a whole and an accurate, objective understanding of one's company should be encouraged. For example, balance must somehow be maintained the more market share rises. This can be accomplished either by the whole company acting towards contributing to society, or by raising its overall ability to provide better service to customers.

Regarding marketing and advertising, the more splendidly one wants to sell one's company, the more should the same scale of attention and budget be directed towards manifesting simplicity and humility. For example, the head office building, and business offices should be designed and furnished with simplicity and modesty. The company should also emphasize prioritizing quality and eliminating superficial appearance in all of its services, products, and operations.

2. Harmony in the Company

Concerning systems and policies that form the ways, culture, and climate of the company, it is necessary to carry out benevolent measures ensuring employees' health, security after retirement, etc. Merit-rating systems and policies are necessary so that appropriate respect can be given to those in the shadow of rising employees as well as to those who are important "supporting players" or those who do valuable work deeper in the background. It is necessary to form policies and systems that foster the kind of atmosphere where those in high positions take good care of those in lower ones. An objective personnel assessment system, which calls for an attitude of modesty and humility especially for personnel with higher positions of management, becomes necessary.

Since this kind of sense of values will be formed from the individual characters of the employees, so top managers themselves should establish an "external advisory committee" as a resource for their own consultation.

Forming the Imperishable Company

EVERYTHING IN THIS WORLD is formed by the nothing-ness of the Tao and finishes its life by returning to nothingness; this is the action of the Tao. It arises from and returns to a weakness that has forsaken strength.

An enterprise also has a fixed life span and proceeds from establishment to growth and then to maturity before returning to nothingness. When this process is followed, the enterprise typically declines after thirty or forty years. But the enterprise must develop, reach fullness, and then continue, so what can be done to achieve this? When the enterprise still has vigor — in transition from growth to maturity — it is desirable to establish it anew. This means reestablishment rather than reform. It is necessary to carry this out with enough clarity to create a fresh start for the company.

Having new people in the "driver's seat" will be man-dated and this will often mean a new president. It is exceed-ingly difficult for the person who has brought growth to the company to act creatively in the destruction of what has been achieved; he or she cannot escape from one's past glories. Therefore, a successor is needed. However, because the successor will show diffidence towards his or her predecessor — especially true in the case of a president — it is difficult to carry out radical changes. The previous president should act as a guardian, granting free rein and allowing her or him to exercise all his or her skills. If things carry on as they are, the prior president's achievements will be returned to nothingness and the only method of preventing this is to carry out establishment of the enterprise anew. Allowing his or her successor to act as she or he sees fit is thus highly beneficial. With the assistance of the previous president, who is the person who made the greatest contribution to the company, the new president will start the company freshly in accordance with then contemporary trends and will put the company back on the road to growth.

It is inevitable that the action of the Tao in life and throughout the world will return it to nothingness. As this poses a serious problem for an enterprise, so a fresh start must be made. If this is the first point, there is also a second, to place primary importance on the things that are in conformance with the action of the Tao.

Regarding people, in trying to make the enterprise eternal, those bearing the burdens of the company must be replaced at regular intervals to allow it to continue. Therefore, the more importance is placed on people, the more smoothly will continuity be achieved. This stands to reason. If one considers that the company exists today because of people who have periodically supported it like relay athletes, then it will be clear how important each former employee is for the present company. Therefore, for those whose period of employment is complete, their contributions should be honored, and especially for retirees, they should be taken care of by setting up systems to assure security in old age and promote health care. If this kind of warm treatment is given to one's predecessors, both those continuing in their positions as well as beginning employees will feel reassured.

A similar situation exists for products. If it is held that past products made the company what it is today, then improving the identity, the special features, and the techniques that went into making those products will come to have great importance.

This tradition of warmly treating the people and products that supported the company for a finite period will, conversely, provide the fundamental strength that will allow the company to maintain eternal continuity.

No. 41 DOH-I

The Twenty-first-century
Management Leader

WHEN THE PERSON of high knowledge and ability listens to the Tao, she or he understands and puts it into practice. But when the person of no merit listens to the Tao, he or she only laughs at it as being something foolish. Just as Truth cannot be called as such unless it can be laughed at, so the prominent person of true excellence is sometimes not recognized as such by others and is, instead, made fun of or rudely mocked.

企業は人なり

It is said, "The enterprise is the people in it." Because the enterprise is a human group, it means that the capabilities of the group are determined by the quality of its people. One leader can heavily affect the destiny of the enterprise. The management philosophy of the enterprise changes greatly according to the leader's human qualities and sense of values, while all other employees, regardless of personal preferences, acquiesce to these changes and diligently continue their work. Over a long period, the changes can make one wonder whether it is still the same company.

Getting a leader of character and insight is good, but if it is a person who is one-sided and acts only through coercion at the slightest chance, as soon as he or she assumes office, the group will undergo severe change becoming a closed, self-seeking one where people will be treated as no more than expendable domestic animals. Even if such a leader leaves, a tremendous amount of time and energy will be required to recover from this situation. In the worst case, the result will be bankruptcy. As a leader gets older, it is extremely difficult for her or him to continue for a long time. The lesson here is: "You don't hang on to success."

There are numerous examples of where a single technician, like the one leader who influences the destiny of the company, decides the future of the enterprise. If we were to ask why a certain company exists today, it is certain that our inquiry would arrive at one distinguished manager and one distinguished technician. Many people would say that like a mad person, this noted technician has devoted most of his or her life's energy to developing new technology. To put it in ordinary language, she or he is an eccentric, an oddball. Such a person finds satisfaction difficult within the confines of the company and seems to defy common sense by continuing to spend his or her days absorbed only in developing technology. Because the rules of the company are not being obeyed, there is criticism. Thus, a superior guardian or person who understands is necessary and it is highly desirable that it be the current manager.

There are many large-scale enterprises without these kinds of people. It is necessary to encourage technicians (and others) to explore new ideas and developments, often those that only prompt laughter from ordinary people. Through such stimulus and support, inventions great enough to change the history of one's company may occur.

To be like this, always in the background giving each employee the chance for her or his talents to bloom and protecting them from obstacles, is the role of the leader.

Getting results and spectacular achievements is the function of each employee; the leader should in no way be conspicuous. However, the employees must always have the desire to achieve the next objectives, achieving results through resolute challenge while leading a life of fulfillment. This kind of group will not meet with deterioration. Thus, this kind of leader is indeed one that should be called a leader of excellence and distinction.

No. 42 DOH-KA

The Secret of Creation
and Bringing Up

THINGS ARE SAID TO BE CREATED BY CHUKI, power generated through the interaction of the twin cosmic forces of Yin (shade) and Yang (light).

The most important thing for an enterprise is creativity. Essentially, the enterprise exists to devise and implement attractive social proposals for the improvement of society and life in general. Its function is to make the kinds of situations that cause us inconvenience and discomfort even a little bit better. When the enterprise generates such social proposals, people who are in favor of them become customers. The enterprise then has to put these proposals into practice and based on this, they have to actually produce products and services.

Often things causing inconvenience and discomfort have remained the same until now because it had been thought that improvement was technically or otherwise impossible. To eradicate this kind of conception is not an easy thing.

However, progress means making the impossible possible. This is where it is important to believe that "it is definitely possible." This is precisely the power of creation, Chuki, the power to make something from nothing.

Initially, if the power to think that something is definitely possible is not present, then nothing will be brought about. Things are produced through the interaction of the twin cosmic forces of Yin (shade) and Yang (light). Thus the interplay of two complete opposites is the source that brings things into being. It is not a case of choosing either Yin or Yang, the concept must consist of both opposites together.

In the case of products, at the level of thinking about function or quality, quality or cost, nothing unique or epoch-making has yet been produced. The idea that includes both is the one that boosts excellence. When we think about it, the wonderful things in this world always include two extreme opposites: i.e., cold and warmth, hardness and softness, and the top athlete is always relaxed but keenly alert. Ideas also should always be the harmony of light and shade. A certain element A clashes with a completely opposite element B forming, in its reconciliation, a third factor previously nonexistent. Therefore, in wanting to form ideas, one element or theme in isolation produces nothing; bringing in a different kind of element is vital. Their interaction will give birth to something fresh and new.

Thinking like this makes us realize how important it is for a corporate organization to have the attitude of placing emphasis on "different kinds of things." Nothing spectacular comes out of a human organization that is of uniform color and nature. If there is no collision of different elements no sparks are formed, there is no ignition, and nothing is produced.

When the state of two opposite extremes blending together in harmonious coexistence is realized, and startling epoch-making products, services, and business exceeding normal common sense will be created.

No. 43 HEN-YOH

The Flexible-Thinking Organization

WHAT IS THE MOST EFFECTIVE KIND OF ORGANIZATION? According to Lao-tzu, nothing is superior to water. Beginning now, we could usefully learn from water how the corporate organization should be.

The best kind of organization is a flexible one. It should be formed freely depending on the theme. Water changes its shape according to the openings it fills, leaving no space. If there is a fixed shape and form this will only be a hindrance to filling spaces, whereas if not fixed, any kind of form will be accommodated and any kind of condition will be swiftly surmounted.

In the group engaged in the production of a film, or the climbing team challenging a virgin peak, depending on the specific themes and conditions each time, it is normal to create a new setup by using different people and by changing the formation itself. However, enterprises lack such freedom, and thus are limited in tackling their work by using the best formation and personnel. This needs to be radically improved. Selection must be made of what kind of personnel with which kinds of abilities are necessary to achieve the desired aims. The personnel with these abilities must then, one by one, be fitted to crucial roles. If no such members are to be found in the company itself, then positions should be filled from outside sources for a certain fixed period. Temporary admission of external ability should also serve to stimulate the activities of those already in the company. When there is a problem for the whole company to overcome, for a limited time all employees will rally to surmount the problem. From the point of view of efficiency, it is much more effective than assigning a few to work on it for a long period.

Thinking along these lines, the work of a company's Management Department should entail computerizing each employee's data. Management of each employee, management of business, financing, management of attendance, wage management, and so forth. should all be computerized. However, if work is still left over, it can be shared with other employees by applying a two-job system, such as a salesperson who also takes care of ceremonial duties, or a developer who also works in social welfare. This will have the result of doubling contributions to the company that will increase employees' satisfaction and become a turning point in producing ideas.

There is also a boundary between internal and external resources. If the rigid, often oppositional relationship of seller and buyer is removed and flexible thinking is introduced, there will be unlimited possibilities. Without establishing the specific post of salesperson, if there really are users who value the products highly, then anybody can be a salesperson and at that moment, such a post becomes limitless. Without specifically establishing the post of developer, if excellent ideas are offered for certain themes or conditions, anyone can be appointed as a member of the development department from a professional development planner with a global focus to an ordinary person with good ideas.

In this way, there is no limitation for the person who practices flexibility in her or his organization. It becomes a mine of possibilities.

No. 44 RITSU-KAI

Fulfilling the Social Role

AMONG HONOR, WEALTH, AND ONE'S BODY, which is the most important? It has to be one's body, but somehow, we place more importance on and give priority to honor and wealth. When this happens, on the contrary, we lose honor and wealth and even our bodies. Without forgetting the spirit of gratitude, we must endeavor to limit our desires and to be moderate in our satisfaction in order to sustain ourselves.

With an enterprise as well, one that is not thorough and is vague about what should be given importance and priority will face increasing danger as the company becomes bigger and what should be stressed will be neglected.

What should the greatest importance be placed upon? Upon the social role of one's company and the organizational fullness that consistently maintains it. When the real social role is not fulfilled and profits are earned by virtue of its name recognition and simply being large scale, the company will gradually lose sight of its true social role. When this happens, it will not be clear as to what kind of new and high-grade technology and/or ability is required to support this role, or they will be way off the mark causing a distancing from what a true enterprise should be. In the end, the corporate body itself is ruined and the result is discontinuation of business and bankruptcy.

The correct way to collect earnings is to never forget one's company's social role and to polish up on the technology and abilities needed to create clear themes that will point to what should be done, and how, in order to better fulfill this role for more people. It is this kind of internal effort that is the company's business and earnings should appear as the results.

Therefore, the task of management should be to steer the interest of the company as a whole in the direction of achieving its social role while promoting the spirit of motivation to improve upon its fulfillment. It should not be forgotten that the enterprise exists for the sake of improving, if only slightly, society and life, and that directing interest, attention, and motivation in this direction constitutes proper corporate activity.

What should be done, and how, to achieve the above? First, it is necessary to thoroughly impress on all employees that they should never forget the company's social role. Especially in board meetings, importance should be placed on monitoring how each department is dealing with this. Next, it is necessary to adjust and prioritize the aims of the company as a whole. Then, it should be determined if customers truly recognize the value of goods and services that are the embodiment of the company fulfilling its social role as well as being the preconditions for sales and profits. Since customers exchange the things of value they have (money) for the results that they have recognized as being of value, thus creating sales and profits, the order of priority thus becomes: value-added ratio, profits, sales.

No. 45 KOH-TOKU

Serenity in a Turbulent Age

THE PERFECT SITUATION looks as if it is lacking something; true eloquence seems to be lacking in fluency; and true dexterity seems to have something of the clumsy about it.

Above all else, the enterprise should take "continuous fulfillment of development" as its ultimate theme. Because the organization achieves fullness and continues to maintain its social role, people wanting to participate in such benefits increase and the company becomes indispensable for them. Indeed, this kind of enterprise continues because of demands for its continuance from society. Therefore, it must not be forgotten that rather than through the assertions of the company itself, it is through the demands of society that the company is maintained. Thus, it is necessary to periodically confirm with customers how the company can best serve society. If it is a sufficiently competent enterprise, then the fundamentals will not be shaken. A true enterprise is one that has clear social roles and continues to perfect their fulfillment. Therefore it becomes important to fulfill social roles through corporate activities themselves, which means that products and services are of utmost significance. Thus, the aim is to earn recognition of one's products and services as being clearly superior to others. There should be no relying on superficiality, bluffing, and showiness through one's own inaccurate claims.

If the company hopes to exist only for a year or two, it can engage in advertising battles and concentrate its energies on obtaining high marks. However, such a company intrinsically has no goal for its existence as an enterprise. Given the precondition of eternal continuity, the company should first plan to build up strength for the long term and to find a method where, under the best of circumstances, its roles can be fulfilled. This is where "serenity" comes in. The opposite of this is frenzy, and rushing around in an agitated state can bring good results for a time but this does not last. Indeed, this kind of energy could be much better directed to fulfilling the main purpose, which is to continuously provide better goods and services than anyone else. Instead of becoming frantic about adverse changes in business conditions and the outside environment, it is much more effective to slowly but surely provide superior goods and services to society, to create even a few extra supporters, and to build a variety of foundations for forming relationships with customers. This is because whatever kind of adverse business conditions there may be, the person who finds the goods and services really necessary will always demand them and in many cases, they will become indispensable to a certain facet of people's lifestyles. This kind of relationship with customers will mean that composure will be retained when there are changes in the business climate.

Thus, the enterprise that sincerely devotes itself to implementing the fulfillment of its social role in serenity will be the one that eventually comes out on top. On a personal level, in turbulent times and when there are multiple threats from the rapidly changing situation, it is also necessary to earnestly strive to carry out one's tasks in a spirit of serenity.

No. 46 KEN-YOKU

Understanding Balance

INSECURITY IN LIFE only leads to insatiable human desire. Because there is no limit to desire that strives for
more, there will only be gain that eventually leads to loss as
the power of balance will be called into action. Thus, if desire is not repressed and one tries constantly to obtain
things from others, in other words if there is no feeling of
"this is enough," then great calamity will be invited.

An enterprise exists in the midst of society made up of
various people with mutual relationships. That is, it exists
because of a certain balance. Therefore, what happens to
the enterprise that thinks of nothing but itself and continues to obtain things one after the other? Eventually, the
company puts its fingers into the pie of others' territories
and possessions. What happens if there is no attention paid
to this kind of error? There will be a situation where one
side only gains while the other only loses. This imbalance
does not last forever. As happens in this world, there is always
a restoring force seeking balance that acts to make the company that has constantly gained suffer eventual reverse and
loss, and this happens because there is no moderation. Or,

to put it another way, there is no force exercised to restrain the desire. Thus, it is necessary to determine the company's territory and to always stay within it while continuing to constantly improve its capabilities, products, and services.

How should growing desire be dealt with? It should be firmly directed towards obtaining the enthusiastic support of customers. The days when an enterprise could take pride in its share of the market are over; instead, pride should be taken in how strongly bonds have been established with each customer. To create customers who are true supporters and sustain the company, it is necessary to forge relationships of close friendship through one's work. A computerized system providing clear information about each customer's appearance, name, preferences, and favorite products should be set up at each sales point, to assist this process.

The foundation of this becomes a spirit of being "thankful to the customer" and "knowing when is enough." The company continues due to the existence of customers who give faithful support and by being thankful to these customers, a desire to improve by trying to make the customers even happier will be created. There is no superficial treatment of customers here, where the number of customers is simply reduced in times of business slumps. What is necessary is a corporate attitude where deep bonds with the customers, and even the kind of strong relationships similar to those that exist between parents, children, and even grandchildren are sought.

Therefore, "knowing when is enough" is important. That which puts the brakes on desire that aims to meddle in what others own is holding the attitude that "for this company's capabilities, this amount of expansion is enough." This in turn will cause energy to be directed towards raising one's company's capabilities. In long-term management planning, the establishment of "expansion in balance with capabilities" and "expansion in balance with closeness with

customers" should be given the greatest attention as important management indicators.

No. 47 KAN-EN

The Enterprise as a High-Grade Human Group

ONE WHO FOLLOWS THE TAO knows what is happening in the world without taking a step outside. He or she knows what is truly important without reference to the external world. Conversely, the more one eagerly rushes to the outside seeking after information, not only will no information of importance be obtained, but one will be only deluding oneself.

The enterprise is the people in it; it is a human group. 「企業は人なり」
Also, customers are humans, which means that the enterprise is wholly made up of relationships with people. Henceforth, a higher level of ability will be called for, but what is this high-level ability?

As the enterprise is comprised of its relationships with people, then the "ability of human relationships" is most essential. Exactly what kind of ability is necessary to improve relationships with people? It is the ability to have insight into people. For human relationships within the company, it is the ability to quickly perceive the nuance of something without relying on instructions from superiors, or else the ability to understand subordinates' opinions and desires, not expressed directly, which are inferred from what is behind what they say and how they act.

The more one excels in this kind of ability, the more will attention be paid to the fullest details of creating human relationships and this will show the power of understanding employees. When people feel that they have been understood they will return respect and have an affinity for the other party, so that the support of everyone in the company will be forthcoming. Even if one such person is added, because this will lead to formation of good human relationships inside the company, or to put it another way, a human group excelling in building human relationships, truly close human relationships will be formed and the power of the organization will be evident. In relationships with customers as well, perceiving what the customer really wants is a starting point of business. This kind of enterprise will be able to respond to latent needs which even the customers themselves did not notice and will become a company with the intelligence to deal with the demands put before it, thus earning the support of a huge number of customers.

Therefore, the root of prosperity of an enterprise is not to be found outside, but within the company, in the heart of each employee. Attention must first be placed on what is happening within the company, and a keen eye must be continuously kept on its situation. Next, are any errors being committed in the work carried out by each employee? Then, do all of these employees possess abilities that enable them to carry out their tasks properly without the need for correction that results in losses? After that, the understanding and perception of a "high-level" person, most of which concerns the ability to firmly grasp that which cannot be seen, must be ascertained.

The digital society means coexisting with computing systems. As the ability of businesspeople has often been weighted in terms of being in charge of computing systems for the high-tech age, some people working at this level may be forced to quit. True human ability will be brought into question and fostering the above kind of ability will become crucial at both the individual and corporate levels.

No. 48 BOH-CHI

Points of Attention
for the Manager

WHAT SHOULD THE MANAGER OR THE LEADER pay attention to? The "continuous fullness of development" is essential.

For this purpose, it is necessary to provide goods and services of unique value that are better than others or do not exist elsewhere.

For this purpose, it is necessary to understand customers' demands.

For this purpose, it is necessary to define the sphere of existence in creating the "Only One company on a global scale."

For this purpose, it is necessary to make sure the company is consistently fulfilling its social role.

For this purpose, unique techniques and abilities are necessary.

For this purpose, it is necessary to have the desire to make the impossible possible for the employees.

For this purpose, it is necessary to have insight into the future as the source of motivation.

It is the role of the manager to put these seven essential points into practice in order to improve results. Then, what should be done to enable the above to be smoothly carried out? To work with people of talent. Sub-leaders are necessary to take responsibility for managing the seven points. It is the role of the leader to ensure that the sub-leaders, while smoothly carrying out their roles, pool their faculties into a collective corporate strength.

What must this kind of leader or manager pay attention to? First, it is not knowledge. The level where knowledge is applied lies within the territory of the sub-leader. Why is this? For example, what will happen if he or she cannot predict movements in the exchange market; cannot anticipate the appearance of new technology; is not aware of disputes within the company; and does not notice that the best technicians are being headhunted by others?

Even if there is an abundance of knowledge, is the person who has absolutely no ability to go beyond this knowledge through "foreseeing" and a "sixth sense" fit to be a manager especially in these difficult and turbulent times? What is now demanded of top management is not the cultivation of knowledge through the efforts of intense study. It is the ability of foreseeing and feeling everything and where there is a feeling of union with the Cosmos. This ability declines the more knowledge is increased; the more knowledge there is, the more confusion is caused. If the Tao is continuously followed, awareness will come of something greater than knowledge. When this happens, knowledge will decrease with a proportionate awakening of a keen sense of foresight. Why should this be so? It is because a state of nonaction will be created. But what is this? One's desire has already gone and there is sincere hope that the whole company and the people concerned pass their days with no problems. Hoping for the best will naturally help the sub-leader to produce results because she or he is supported behind the scene. Thus, the actual manager, i.e., the leader, tends to pay attention and work more behind the scene.

Therefore, if a leader's actions are conspicuous, he or she is straying away from the role and reason of a true leader, and sooner or later that will lead to a difficult situation.

TAO Management

No. 49 NIN-TOKU

Professional Groups

S AINTS DO NOT POSSESS PERSISTENT THOUGHTS. It is
said that they make the hearts of those appointed
from above their own. In other words, they do not cling to
their own opinions, but rather they do things in sympathy
with the feelings of the majority of the people.

"Sustaining full development," i.e., good, smooth progress should be given the utmost consideration by companies. The best way to achieve this is by not becoming too
shackled to the past and by not clinging to a small number
of ideas.

On these points, it is necessary to take a fresh look at
the relationship between the company and the employee.
Until recently, organizations have considered not how employees disrupt order, but rather how they keep the various
company rules, as a deciding factor in helping the company
to run smoothly. Why? Because, thanks to the legacy of mass
production and mass sales, the first principle of business
has been the pursuit of efficiency through uniformity.

What about now? Companies already seem to be moving towards the next stage, and the first principle of this stage is "creativity."

We have reached the age of small volume, diversified product production, and "made-to-order allowing choice." Today, in an age of local production and sales based on made-to-order requests and assembled from a wide variety of patterns and colors, parts, and products chosen according to one's individual preference, what supports the "inspiration and creativity" providing this variety? In this kind of age, it should not be that employees observe the rules set by the company, but that the company observes the rules agreed upon by the employees.

Formerly, company rules and regulations existed "so that work was carried out smoothly." The person who knows best whether or not work is going smoothly is the person in charge of it. Therefore, they themselves should create the guidelines or systems that will bring ongoing results. Particularly systems to do with personnel — and within that, systems to do with their treatment — should be such that they easily reap results; accordingly there should be big changes of both work type and the personality of a company. Therefore, a "natural system" should be created by those employees who must observe it, through consensus.

Formerly, the ideal was not to have any regulations in a company. This was because within the attributes of the professional, natural systems were already integrated in order to smoothly obtain results. Consequently, the more an employee continues his or her pursuit of professionalism, the more regulations decrease and are simply observed independently. It is now time for companies to expand that definition and become conscious of the kind of professionalism that can be found in other genres of human groups such as professional orchestras and sports teams.

If one's purpose as an organization is clearly stated, and one's own role for successfully achieving these ends is clearly defined, one should be able to do the work involved in carrying out this role independently and without the need for monitoring by others.

It is time for "self-respecting companies" to start appearing in earnest. Employees can concentrate solely on carrying out their own roles as they themselves have decided on them. Further, there will be a great expansion in the organization's results through the results contributed by each individual. This is how future companies ought to be:

> Just as each member of an orchestra completes his or her own practice in order to excel at one's own part, and then comes together with the others, this time to rise to the challenge of the full ensemble, so should the company of the future function.

> Just as each person in a film production team perfects the preparations for her or his own role, then joins together with the others to create new and combined value in facing the real thing, so should the company of the future function.

No. 50 KI-SEI

Companies with Respect for Life

LIFE COMES OUT OF THE TAO revealing itself in this world as a figure. Death is the entering into the Tao and the extinguishing of the figure. Since there is no essential difference between the two, neither is cause for great sorrow nor great joy. Even though one is born to have a long life, one is paring away one's longevity.

A company should seize its opportunities as an "assembly of life." When people — who receive life in this world, are brought up with the keen hopes of their parents, and spend their youth with devoted support from many — finally reach maturity having completed their instructional period, the stage they stand upon is the company. In some cases, the majority of the energy in one's life is spent on one's company. On consideration of this, we realize how irreplaceable the company really is for humans.

The overall attitude of the company thus becomes vastly more significant. It must enthusiastically undertake a broader range of considerations, from the awareness that the company consumes that most precious thing called life, to how much it wishes to help the lives of its own employees blossom and provide them with contented lives.

Of the greatest importance is "the provision of a life plan." Each individual employee has her or his own characteristic life unlike anyone else. However, if they are not careful, they can end up living in employee dormitories, spending the majority of the day at work, eating all three meals in the company canteen, and thus spending their days in a very nonindividual way. There are surprisingly large numbers of people who don't realize this until they have reached retirement.

Richness is to have choices in plenty. An enriched life is one where we can live each day off a "special menu" that can only be lived by us, having chosen from amongst a wealth of options. To achieve this, we first need to draw a life plan that outlines how we want to spend our days and the kind of goals we are aiming for.

Secondly comes "the provision of opportunity development." Self-advancement and the development of one's potential are nurtured. Arrangements are made whereby an employee has these kinds of opportunities in the different aspects of her or his life. Provisions must also be made for an "educational training program" in order to foster the capability of employees to make full use of such opportunities.

As a final objective, the company should either appoint the executives who will take office, or with the support of the company, become independent and function as a venture business, establishing those who will act as managers. It can choose to work in the city and act as the head office, or to locate in the countryside and do factory or other manufacturing work. Either way, if the income generated is enough to cover living costs, then housing and living conditions are provided for.

What are such companies called? "Companies with respect for life." It is these kinds of companies that earn the reputation of being life partners for their employees, in which they can relax and take time in coming to grips with their jobs.

On the other hand, the right mental attitude on the employee's side is equally important. That is the awareness that careers, riches, and honors are not all there is to life. A truly enriched life is "a life that only I can live."

With a typical career, when one ends up as president or director, the majority of one's life will be spent in devoting all one's time in competition, concentrating solely on survival. When one looks back, what is left?

How should our own unique lives be and how should the companies that will act as the main stages of this life interact? Now, the time has come when both company and employees should consider the company with a view to its placing increased emphasis upon the quality of the human lives it sustains.

The Creative System

ALL THINGS THAT EXIST IN THIS WORLD have been produced by the Tao, have revealed forms trained by Virtue, and have been raised by the power of Nature.

Further, as the Tao produces all things, this means that they do not belong to us. Even if we have made that thing, we must not hold or rely upon it. Even if we grow something we must not control it. This deep mystery, which without personal attachment appreciates the substance made or grown, is the core essence of Virtue.

Companies are the production source of things. If there are no systems within the constituents of the company for producing and nurturing the work through to the end product or service, as well as the requisite talent and cash flow, then the company will not produce results. Rather, we can say that the power of a company lies in whether or not its administration is managed smoothly. Despite there being no more important process than this, why is it that companies do not try to investigate or clarify it?

Lao-tzu is clear. He cogently asserts the metaphysical action that accompanies people's creative ability or growth potential. First, nothing can live without the help of the Tao. Second, without the action of Virtue nothing can begin its process towards sensitivity, and there can be no development of shape or form. Further, nothing can be completed without the help of Nature's powers. In other words, for companies — whose work is to produce and complete things — nothing can be produced without the harmony of these three things, "the force of the Tao, the action of Virtue, and the power of Nature."

Of particular importance is the action of Virtue. No matter that one has plenty of ideas; to finally turn that seed of an idea for a new product or service into a sound end product is tough. The strength to break through this great difficulty is provided by the action of Virtue.

So, what kind of a thing is Virtue? It is the attitude of not regarding something as one's own even though one has produced it, not anticipating success, and not trying to control something even though one has helped it to grow and develop. In other words, there is not the faintest element of the sentiment, "for one's own desire." To put it another way, the pleasure of producing and nurturing something is derived solely from the happiness of others. Once that is over, one moves on to the next topic.

Why? Because one has already passed the process of giving pleasure through production; the "skin" of the business or product has already been shed, its satisfaction having been gained. Since excitement and new joy can not be felt by remaining permanently at that point, the view that it is better to move on promptly to the next topic is justifiable. In other words, the value is in the very process; there is no real value in having attained fame and name or in having achieved high growth.

The spirit of the inaugurator asserts the above. Yet for him or her to remain seated at the top for many years, continuing to exert control until being thought of as an old obstacle, is due cause for the spirit of the former inaugurator to weep.

During the company's inauguration period and growth, the inaugurator is someone who thinks, "Forget about the self," wishes only for growth along with the times, and absorbs himself or herself single-mindedly in the work of the company. However, once the company settles at a certain scale and the inaugurator begins to feel her or his age, one eventually comes to live dependent on personal control of the company that she or he established, on hierarchy and success. Since this attitude is the antithesis of how Virtue should be, no great business or products will be produced from that point on and the company will simply hover where it is.

These kinds of conditions may also arise because the company is opposing the ways of the Tao and Virtue. If the company wishes to become unstuck and grow anew, then the best solution is for the inaugurator to promptly step aside and for the ways of the Tao and Virtue to be restored.

✻

No. 52 KI-GEN 起源

The Key to Management Success
— The Application of the Tao

WHAT IS THE THINKING that shapes the basis of this Tao Management? Ultimately it is the following:

> The Tao is the mother that produces all things. We already appreciate that each one of us is a child born from this mother. If we remember this and observe the way of the Tao that is the mother, we shall find stability in our lives.

If one thoroughly understands the essence and the main points of this way of thinking, then one will be able to manage a business with ease. Despite this, almost all managers tread a path of suffering. They struggle desperately for secure conditions to come along.

So, what are the main points of Tao Management? First, one should realize that one's own abilities and capacity are negligible.

In which case, what should one do? One needs to gain the cooperation of many others.

156   TAO Management

How can that be gained? Initially we have only our own poor abilities. However, by bringing one's own abilities and capacities to full power, one can win the cooperation of others. People who put their whole heart into living have people supporting them who also put their whole life into living. However, it is clear that things do not run well on this alone.

Absolutely indispensable information, i.e., business communications or customers, arrives with the best possible timing. Or, information sought for a long time — like highly specific technology or solutions — happens to turn up at an unexpected moment. Perhaps these really can be attributed to "the action of the heavens" or "good luck." We 神技・運 deeply understand the absolute importance of "management" that transcends ordinary kinds of logic. Indeed, if business management is not tinged, to a certain extent, with timing that surpasses human wisdom or strong luck, its power will not appear.

What is this "management"? It is "the actions of the Tao and Virtue" as explained by Lao-tzu. Knowledge is only knowledge. In other words it has limits because it is acquired only with one's head. Because it has not been acquired with the whole body, i.e., it has not been obtained through personal experience, there are times when it can indeed be harmful.

As Lao-tzu especially calls to our attention, since truth is something to be mastered and something that can only be acquired, superficial and half-baked knowledge obstructs 表面だけの and denies the mastering of truth. Truth can only be learned 未熟な from the master — "the actions of the Tao and Virtue." Mere 知識 knowledge can be harmful as well as useless. We must not forget this.

No. 53 EKI-SHOH

Twenty-first-century-style
Top Management

LEADERS WHO WIELD GREAT POWER that controls the lives of many are incompetent without such aware-ness. Those who are dressed in fine clothes and devote themselves primarily to their luxurious lifestyles, although they can enjoy such luxury only at the sacrifice of the valu-able lives of many other people, are called Toko, which means those who steal from others but are proud even so. In human terms, they become people reduced to the level of common thieves.

Businesses reflect the character of their top manage-ment be they great or small in stature. Their members, forms, and presentation exert a large influence on shaping the attitude of the business. Accordingly, top management must first see their company as no different from their own personality. If top management is simple, honest, and sturdy, the atmosphere in its company will follow in the same vein. Top management must not forget that they are public figures representing a group of many people, and are no longer simply individuals. At all times, the job demands conduct based on one's self-awareness as such a public figure.

For the employees, the executives' attitudes in action and the results of their actions are more easily understood than using one million words of explanation. If it is transmitted paradoxically, then nothing need be explained. It is better simply to show through one's own actions.

But, what happens with businesses whose top ranks are constantly in flux? It would be strange if there were no confusion at all since the most important and influential model keeps shifting and changing. The situation would be graver still if there was no confusion; it would be proof that the employees no longer had total faith in their management. The employees would have given so-called "false allegiance" to their employers and a honne, tatemae relationship would exist between them. Can companies with this kind of relationship existing between top management and employees really become first-rate businesses with sustained growth in the long term?

So, what is the role of top management? Of course it must try to achieve "sustained, full development" of the company, to improve on today's business performance, and to make all arrangements to ensure that such company performance can be continued tomorrow. But, who actually carries out these plans made by top management? It is the employees.

In other words, an enterprise is comprised of the work of top management and employees in collaboration with each other. Further, executives do not hold their positions because of their self-designated greatness; rather they hold those positions because they are most fit for that role.

Thus, the position is not for the purpose of throwing one's weight around.

The position is not for creating one's own personal fortune.

The position is not so one can dress in fine clothes and live a life of luxury.

It is simply a position one is engaged in to perform a role.

Any top management that remembers this is extremely likely to see its business develop fully.

❖

No. 54 SHU-KAN 習慣.

The Trick of Not Giving in
to Temptation

人形成

WELL-FORMED PEOPLE ARE INVINCIBLE. Fully-embracing people are indomitable. For people who have truly established the Tao deep within themselves, those teachings can never be drawn out of them. For those who truly and firmly embrace the heart of the Tao, it will never abandon or separate from them no matter what temptations they may come across on the outside. The descendants of these people will end up following the Tao and Nature.

Along the way of a business that carries on for a long time, temptations may show up that threaten its continuation. The biggest of these are the "lucrative stories" of getting large revenues from precious little in the way of effort or labor. Of course it is not going to be quick and easy to make revenues from the value created and offered by the company. At times, work is likely to be interrupted for a while. This means turnover drops, it is harder to make a profit, and the company ends up having financial difficulties. If, at such a time, the invitation came along to simply invest some capital and that capital would multiply without having to expend any effort, what would you do? Against your better judgment, you would probably want to jump aboard.

An investigation of bankrupt businesses reveals that a major portion of them had experienced the very best of periods at one time. Conditions where the winds blow in one's favor and things go well whatever the company does, do not happen often. But it is during this very favorable period that the essence of the enterprise is revealed, and companies may start on the path to failure.

If the regular work is forgotten amidst all the speculation, and if the businesses' duty of continuing the supply of value in the form of an excellent product or service is forgotten, the company will be paralyzed by its foolishness wherein only calculations of turnover rise. It is similar to the procurement of vitality by means of drugs as gradually the core rots away, starting from the roots and then spreading to the main body.

One would think that this is obviously unreasonable behavior, but market changes and conditions can be frightening things. People who are forced into a tight corner often lose their judgment of what is rational. Occasionally large, first-rate companies launch and are unsuccessful at irrational activities that even a child would recognize as such. So, it is a temptation.

There are plenty of temptations even in one's daily work. A frequently occurring case is the temptation to buy the clients' product as a condition to commence trade. If one thinks about it calmly, the customer — who is the buyer — will not recognize the absolute null value of this service, and even should this kind of relationship be entered into, it will never be possible to have a good relationship. Further, we should realize that the moment such conditions are entered into, the precious thing of creating and providing value — that is the very duty of a business — is abandoned and it will be a big blow to the company's work thereafter. Nevertheless, companies inadvertently step onto this track at times of worsening results and they end up treading a path that is impossible to sustain. Consequently, an enterprise should continually reconfirm its duty and the fundamental ideas that define its true role, and should encourage these ideas to permeate deeply into the heart of each and every employee.

Further, a business needs to make sure that there is no unreasonable conduct big enough to rock the whole company that could suddenly appear. This may arise from the resultant "compilation" of previously overlooked items in the details of daily work. Instead of dismissing a problem area with, "It's so trivial, it's not worth it," or "It's nothing important," it is vital to remove it decisively, "Precisely because it is so small."

This nurtures the doctrine, "Well-formed people are invincible. Fully-embracing people are indomitable."

No. 55 GEN-PU

Companies with Vigor

LAO-TZU SOUGHT THE IDEAL HUMAN IN INFANTS. Inno-cent as it is, it is not bitten by poisonous insects, at-tacked by savage animals, nor swooped on by birds of prey. It is known that in times of danger, their bodies are safe. Even though the bones of infants are light, and their mus-cles are flexible, their hands that take grip of something are firm. Even though infants are still unaware of the sexual in-tercourse between man and woman, yet the infants' genitals may be responsive or erect thanks to the completeness of an infant's spirit. Even if an infant has been crying the whole day, its voice is not damaged due to the perfect peace of an infant's mind. Grown-ups have desires and plan events, yet the attraction of returning to the world of one's infant age dwells deep in the mind.

Organizational energy is what an enterprise needs for its activities. An enterprise without strength cannot get through simple obstacles or problems. Vigor produces vigor, and gains one advantage after the next, which is indis-pensable for the activities of an enterprise.

Simply, vigor is the energy of a group. The group energy is the blend of energy radiated by every employee of the company. One could say that the most significant duty of the managers is to plan the application and utilization of this group energy without waste.

In order to achieve this, they must first "focus." The energy of each employee that is emitted randomly in any or all directions is of small value if their combined energy does not exceed that of each individual. It is a powerful thing if the energy of all employees is directed towards the same point. By doing so, the possibility of making a breakthrough even in a case with difficult hurdles, increases. Consequently, there is a need for a vision and a common company goal.

ハードルが高くても

社内共通のゴール

Efficiency is high if the majority of the employees combine efforts to focus daily on one point using the principle "one day-one focus." Results that exceed expectations can be achieved. Good examples of this can be found in orchestras, soccer teams, and movie-production teams. With adoption of the principle "one day-one focus," businesses may also conduct high-level expansion.

「一日　　」

Next, an important aspect of group energy is "wastefulness," and to avoid it managers should reexamine their basic attitudes. What are the conditions where people expend their energies in the most wasteful way? Anxieties caused by "suspicions" and "needless worrying" waste energy. "Anger, fear, and sadness," if in excess, are destructive and there is nothing to compensate for the energy robbed by them.

エネルギーをついやす.

不要な心配

Industry itself is made up of human groups. It is a place where a rich diversity of spirits collides. Therefore, unless much careful thought and attention is given to encouraging a "healthy environment," outbreaks of unproductive energy soon result.

What is a "healthy environment"? It is the internal system where unused energy is not wasted, but where the employees have abundant positive energy to fulfill the "vision"

健全工環境

and "common company goal" or to achieve "today's objectives and assignments" based upon them.

For this purpose, beginning with the company's top executives, managers should take additional care with their way of speaking and behavior in order to avoid "unwanted emotions" that could grow into doubts. They must not let employees' energy be directed at "internal procedures" but to the contrary, they should adjust the company's daily environment so that all energy is directed at the very creation and provision of value itself, and if even minor anxieties are encountered, they should be immediately dealt with and thoroughly dissipated.

TAO Management

No. 56 GEN-TOKU

Work Builds the Rings
of Sympathetic Response

A REALLY WISE MAN OR WOMAN says little and does not fall into temptation. He or she does not make challenging statements and does not behave in a way as to show off his or her abilities. Generally, such a one listens to a voice inside oneself and blames one's own way of doing things as the reason for problems encountered, and there is no room for the world's temptations to enter. Therefore, such a one cannot be readily used by others or precipitate any losses. This is a type of person whose existence is to be respected.

An enterprise has to establish a social existence for itself. Through fulfilling its social obligations the enterprise must make itself an indispensable part of society. Should the company decide "to terminate activities now," how great would be the voice from society, which relies upon its continuation and opposes the closure of the business, that would say "this is a problem for us."

The very basics of the company's social role must be reconsidered yet again if its competitor is known to be able to quickly fill any gap opened by the company. After all, management is a process of daily efforts for the gradual improvement of the company's social role. At all times, listening to the voice inside is very important.

Extend the field of the company's social role. Or increase the number of completed targets. In other words, the people who respond with sympathy to the completion of this role are the company's clients, and increasing their number brings growth in sales. Further, extending turnover would increase the number of sympathetic respondents. With human beings, the more essential the thing, the less effort will be necessary to promote a sympathetic response. If a person is one who possesses originality of thinking, originality of standing, and originality of taste, such a one can become an indispensable supplier.

It is vital to become a "unique company" and to expand the number of sympathetic respondents on global scale. The time of such great opportunities has arrived. The Internet and CALS (Continuous Acquisition and Lifecycle Support, formerly Computer-Aided Logistical Support) are available, and a message can be transmitted almost instantaneously now.

The mechanism of fortune is to "spread goods that assert originality on a global scale." A few centuries ago, people crossed seas and went over mountains in life-risking journeys in order to increase the number of sympathizers even by one. Now it is possible to market through a computer from home. Those who can skillfully take advantage of this convenience can make a fortune.

Yet, as a prerequisite to this, there is one more important question: "What to market?" What is there that can only be carried out at this company and that could be marketed worldwide to as many people as possible? It is in finding this answer that all energies should be invested; thus, the most significant duty of the company's management is "to listen every day to the voice from within."

No. 57 JIN-PU

Twenty-first-century
Ripple Enterprises

THE EARTHLY WORLD IS NOT IDLE, and there is nothing
better to be guided by than the way of the nature,
abandoning all artificial thoughts. Consider the artificial
construct of a prohibition — a tool that is too convenient
and unnecessary. he more such artificiality is esteemed, the
greater the abuses. The more strict laws and ordinances are
installed, the more people will disobey the prohibitions and
commit crimes like robbery.

What direction should a company follow?

It should launch out in a direction that leads to the creation of "a company established not as traditional organization." This needs a person with an idea that is growing and
who intends to fulfill it, i.e., an entrepreneur or an
inaugurator. Like enlarging rings made by a stone tossed
into a pool of water, the assertion or intention proposed by
this person to society ripples in an ongoing expanding cir-

cle; this creates the company's organizational structure and its growth.

The first ring (circle) is likely to be composed of closely related people who are the first sympathetic respondents. They constitute the first investors, occasionally the first clients, and the first employees. Soon enough the assertion is passed on by these people to a second circle, a ring of sympathetic respondents is formed, and these people also become shareholders, clients, and employees. This is the way the ripples widen. By the time the tenth and eleventh circles are formed, they will probably expand well beyond the company's boundaries.

However, these people are not just clients. Concurrent with being passionate customers, they are also enthusiastic salespersons as well as being deeply comprehending shareholders. In this way the ripples serve to expand the structure on a global scale, to the most distant corners of the planet, and then, before long they return. At this point, the ardent voices of many sympathizers may be heard by those who initiated the company.

There is no longer a clear division between "what is within the company" and "what is outside the company." Thus, to a certain extent the distinction between customers and salespersons is meaningless. All of the concerned people are important and all of them are part of the structure. They are all indispensable colleagues who fulfill the social duties of a company. The higher and wider the social obligations that are fulfilled, the greater the number of sympathetic respondents and the scale of expansion.

At this point there is nothing that can be added to the scale of the company. Rather, what is vital is the eagerness and independence of each individual. All of the people are participating independently. Thus, there is no need to bind them by rules. In such an enterprise, structure is important but rules are not.

What is the source of independence, the source of desire? Of course, their incomes, yet, it is not only about money. Rather, satisfaction and fullness from fulfilling one's social obligations brings about a greater delight.

No. 58 JUN-KA

統化
順化
?

Minus and Plus Are Sides
of One Coin

WHEN A DISASTER IS FEARED a fortune approaches; when a fortune is anticipated a disaster is lurking — it is a fact; nobody knows the final outcome. Similarly, a normal thing turns into a mystery and an upright thing becomes something suspicious. How much time do we humans lose in this relative world before we find the right way?

   In the activities of a business, not knowing what will be fortuitous is a common anxiety. Even the harsh claim of a customer can create a closer relationship than before, if high appreciation is received for the brilliant solution that is found. It is not uncommon that due to the failure of a study on the development of a new material, the course of research is altered, and the kind of major product that happens only once in ten years is successfully produced.

   There are also many cases like the following example: all companies in a given industry advance together but one company from an adjacent sphere of business is late to start. This company prepares itself to bear the severe losses of being late to start when, due to changes in social conditions, the market becomes bewitched with bad loans, leaving only the late-to-start company unhurt. Therefore, human wisdom clearly falls far short of grasping the cause and effect relationship of phenomenon like good and ill luck or the weal and woe of life.

A company's accomplishment — marking the conclusion of striving to give the best in one's business activities — lies in a sphere that is beyond human comprehension. Further, a leader should not first divide events into "good and ill luck" and "weal and woe" and then insist on acknowledging just one of each pair, but should always combine them and comply with them both. In other words, they should always work with the knowledge that even if everything is running smoothly, perhaps there is an aspect that might turn the success into failure. For instance, due to a smoothly running operation, the person in charge overestimates a situation or even ignores aspects of it, when they should be keenly on alert for anything that might bring disaster.

On the other hand, even if a company's affairs are not progressing as planned and failures are consequently occurring, they should utilize a broad viewpoint to identify any single aspect that could be taken as a merit and turn the whole process into a success. Thereby, the human values of the leaders are appraised through their ability to pay special attention to the concepts of this theory of relativity as they play out in the larger business world.

The leader must also be careful in the appraisal and evaluation of his or her employees. It is no longer right to create an atmosphere focused solely upon the failings of any employee. Rather, it is important to actively provide employees with more opportunities for them to stretch their merits and show their abilities.

Why? A company is a place that earns income. Put another way, it is a place for making profit, and concurrently it is also a place where people are awakened to the self.

There are different levels of this awakening of the self. There are plenty of cases where people take steps after having become aware of the vast possibilities that could have grown whilst they were sleeping. There are also cases not of becoming aware of this by oneself, but discovering that one can have a very fruitful relationship in cooperation with another person. Therefore step-by-step through business activities, one becomes aware of one's own abilities and eventually demonstrates them. This is another purpose of business.

Day by day the abilities of a company's employees are discovered, demonstrated, and broadened, thus leading to an expansion of that company's capacity that results in an improvement of its business achievements. Such an enterprise knows no decline. In any case "the company becomes a person" as an enterprise is comprised of the conduct of all of the people within.

For this purpose, management must aid and promote the demonstration of employees' virtues. Moreover, the provision of new and challenging opportunities for employees on a daily basis brings rewards over and above a cash income.

No. 59 SHU-DOH

The Trick of Invulnerability

ECONOMY IS THE BEST APPROACH to successfully running everything, for the reason that if resources and energy are ordinarily used economically, and if resources are not completely consumed, recovery is quick. The quicker the recovery, the more ongoing operations are possible while maintaining the constant reserves. This is the so-called deep stabilization of the foundations and is the basis for a long, youthful life.

Certainly an enterprise should also have an extensive and productive life. The basic theory of the long, youthful life that Lao-tzu expounds is also a basic theory of company management. The chief point is that in order to avoid "using up" resources, daily consideration of economy should be made. However, the general rule of up to 70 percent use of resources should not be forgotten. Thus, 30 percent is left, and soon this can easily reach 50 percent, i.e., half. Once numbers have reached half, the possibility of it predominating at 60 percent or 70 percent grows greater.

Let's take the situation where the remaining volume of resources is zero. Once all entire reserves are spent, zero

and one are like "have" and "have not," making the difference very significant. One must first break through this, and
undoubtedly it will require great effort.

Even reaching 10 percent of reserves is a long way off
50 percent, the halfway mark. However, what should be
done if progress is made in small steps, the company is in a
difficult condition, and a great challenge is approaching?
The difference in the future stability of the company between having resources at 30 percent and at 0 percent
should be deeply engraved into the company psyche. That
is why economy is the key to management.

Creating an attitude of "quick recovery" is also important. This means avoiding the creation of a gap for competitors to probe and enter. In this case the competitors are not
only customers and competitive industries but also depres-
sion and economic crisis. Thus, the ideal enterprise always
has just enough provisions of energy and resources to enable it to escape difficulty by itself, no matter how the surrounding environment has changed.

How to create an enterprise with the ability to make a
"quick recovery" is of prime importance. Indeed, this is also
called "invulnerability." If there is such a superb ability available, no matter the magnitude of the inflicted damage, the
enterprise will not die.

Recovery means return to the condition of an abundance of financial resources and energy, i.e., always having
extra "capacity." This is where the power of recovery is often
felt first. To expect growth in an enterprise without such
power is a dubious prospect.

If one makes a new investment, utilizing all of what little one has, and if it fails and all is lost, the rate of success of
subsequent activities would be extremely low, whatever
they might be. On the contrary, if the same new investment
is conducted with a margin and room for maneuver, the entire fund could be monitored, and even include plans for
funds to be withdrawn if needed. In circumstances where

failure is absolutely not tolerated, the probability of failure occurring is high. On the other hand, if a retreat was necessary and if it was handled with margin and room for maneuver, such an activity would proceed smoothly.

Thus, utilizing the "economy" of an entire company as a means of guiding as well as controlling its elements should not be forgotten.

No. 60 KYO-I

Management that Understands the Philosophy of the Universe

IT IS SAID THAT A PERSON WHO LIVES ACTIVELY within the Tao also can not be harmed by the wielding of the devil's mysterious power. This is not because the devil is short of vigorous power, but because this mysterious power cannot harm such a person. Action that is beyond human comprehension can be represented by "the strength or hardness of fate." Apparently evil events such as disasters and/or adversities that strike suddenly without reason frequently occur. One way of restricting this impact is to keep in mind the very existence of both unhappiness and the Tao.

The ultimate gain of living with the understanding of the Tao is that there would not be uncertainty. Such fears produced by superstitions like the devil and Satan are included in this category. Thus, if we have a deep understanding of the philosophy of this universe through the teachings of the Tao, uncertainties like superstitions would vanish. Misfortune and calamity that supposedly "happen because they are like that" would not strike. There are indications and predictions of such impending events. Reading these correctly helps in coping with situations and avoiding damage. In other words, misfortune and calamity take place due to one's disregard, dismissal, or underestimation of the omens or predictions that have already indicated their approach.

With the Tao, anything is possible. Since the self is a fragment of the Tao, by gaining a deep awareness of one's self, one can cultivate this perception. Therefore, as there is no uncertainty in the workings of the Tao, if a call for one's serious attention is not neglected, the whole picture can be seen clearly. Potential damage can then be dealt with and avoided before one is hurt.

Let's take a look at where misfortune occurs. It falls on deliberate things, adds measures unnecessarily, and stirs up the matter. It is said that to govern a big country is like cooking small fish — one should avoid adding extra spices and stirring things up needlessly. The bigger the project, the less should be the unnecessary involvement and disrespect of those associated in order to have a smooth running operation.

Conducting smooth management in an enterprise is just like that. Adding too many rules and strategies and/or frequently changing the responsible people or established systems brings about confusion and mistrust among the related personnel, and an opposite effect is achieved.

What should be done? A main factor related to a project, task, business, or work always exists. This is the essential without which the whole structure cannot be. The point is that if a breakthrough cannot be made here, success will not follow. First, the whole of this has to be analyzed and fully grasped.

The way of grasping a subject is to take a look at the entire project quietly, without artificiality or selfishness. If matters are progressing smoothly, or if you suppose that there are areas progressing smoothly, the reasons for this will surface naturally. This is the main factor of success.

In the process of finding out the gist, the closer you get to the main factor, the more naturally apparent the method of attaining that factor would also become. Having once attained this, nothing else should be added. After this, efforts must be made to create an environment that helps those carrying out the work to proceed easily with their duties.

A leader is not a person who jumps from one struggle into another. Naturally calm and self-possessed, a leader rejects extraneous artificiality and directs efforts towards the creation of a natural and selfless working environment. Further, a leader does not intervene unnecessarily in the working process.

No. 61 KEN-TOKU

Twenty-first-century Enterprises Are Symbiotic Networks

BY **DISCERNING ONE'S DUTY** and identifying what one truly desires, it often turns out that what one desires is unexpectedly easy and insignificant. These desires can all be satisfied if all people act modestly towards each other. Especially with a bigger country or larger company, modesty is even more essential in order to steadily accomplish the genuine hope for a "calm and safe way of life for its citizens or employees."

What true desire should company management harbor? It would be the desire for "continuation."

There is no end for a company, nor can it cease activities. Further, forced termination, i.e., bankruptcy, is out of the question. It has its part in the social system, so even its inaugurators cannot treat the company as something that belongs to them. Yet, just securing continuation is not good enough. The responsibility of management requires "full development," i.e., taking on a high level of social obligations and further expanding them. Therefore, "sustained, full development" is the true desire that company management ought to possess.

Straying from this true desire or true hope leads to expansionist attempts that often use unexpectedly aggressive and extremely forceful methods, typically causing a situation impossible to sustain. Thus, if a company's executives managed to attain sustained, full development during their term of office, they may be regarded as being successful.

So, what is the other attitude necessary in order to attain this? "Humility."

Quarrels do not grow from a humble attitude. What grows is a peaceful coexistence. If sustained, full development means that the related people and society coexist peacefully together, then this strongly indicates to the managers just how important a humble attitude is.

Humility is not aimed only at customers. There is also a need to create a "symbiotic feeling" towards stock and purchase lines, for they are also like customers. The creation of this "symbiotic network" structure in conjunction with all parties involved is a major factor enabling the company to sustain its full development. In fact, it will become the fundamental idea of corporate management from this point forward.

A symbiotic network structure formed through the humble attitude of interested parties can be directed at potential customers before long — the people who will be future interest groups. Further, the more consideration is given to expanding the symbiotic network on a global scale, the more thorough the humble attitude becomes, and the less room remains for rival ways of thinking. The target of the symbiotic network should be expanded beyond humans to encompass the natural environment and the Earth itself.

Symbiotic networks should exist as the obvious way of thinking for a harmonious interrelationship between companies, the natural environment, and the Earth as a whole. If the company devotes itself to this "symbiosis," it will induce the most efficient use of inputs — since they will gain products and materials — and reconcile all the components that make up the activities of the business. Additionally, confrontations will tend to disappear, eliminating difficulties and allowing smooth progress.

Although this is only one element of corporate activity, if smooth progress is attained through the harmony that is achieved by such symbiotic observance, then naturally downturns in business results across the whole scope of activities can be minimized. It may indeed be concluded that this is the best way to guide a business to sustained, full development.

No. 62 I-DOH

Open-mindedness and Prudence

WHY DID THE ANCIENT PEOPLE think the Tao is precious? They knew that understanding the Tao not only enabled them to achieve what they were searching for, but also thought that the Tao could help one to grow beyond his or her sins. Its focus was not to judge whether or not a sin was committed, but to judge whether its commands were obeyed or not. For in the philanthropic spirit of the Tao was felt an absolute existence on an immeasurable scale, which asked not about crimes committed in the past, but whether the Tao was being obeyed in the present.

The spiritual basis an enterprise requires also necessitates an open mind, free of meanness. 必要とする

Undoubtedly, there is a concern to not supply company products to crime-tainted people. While aiding or otherwise supporting criminals is illegal, is it right to single out customers who have committed crimes in the past and refuse to sell them products? Surely what we should be questioning is their present state of affairs and actions.

By extension, is it right to permanently restrict activities with a company based on the fact that it had committed a crime at some time in the past? It would be a sad loss of an excellent enterprise if such a company that had committed crimes in the past, had woken up to its social responsibilities, imposed strict self-examination, adopted a proper style, and turned into a normal and decent company, to then be permanently haunted by the burden of its past crimes and left only with the option of retreating from the Tao. Instead, the company should be judged by its current state of affairs.

The same goes for the relationship between a company and its employees. Obviously, employees who commit crimes of magnitude have to be fired. They are not the subjects of this discussion. The question is rather how much to try to assist employees who continue, and whether it is really fair to restrict their promotion because of past misdeeds. It is especially important to give generous treatment to, and keep watch over, employees who have inflicted losses on the company.

We frequently hear the expression, "failure is the mother of success" and that the failure itself is a valuable experience. The problem lies in the employee's attitude after the mistake. First, has the employee examined his or her wrongdoing deeply? Second, what has the employee learned from his or her wrongdoing? What's more, how has the company used that mistake as a lesson to alter the way things are presently? In other words, it is not about judging past misdeeds but about making changes for the better.

The company must accrue experience from the past in order to act with greater dynamism thereafter, and must make its social contributions today more dynamic by looking ahead to the future. Therefore, to gain the dynamism necessary to heighten, broaden, and deepen the function for self-examination of normal corporate behavior and the social function of the firm, the company must exist in an internally and externally unified form as either one body or interlinked pair.

It is not a difficult managerial decision regarding how to treat an employee who has failed in his or her duties and inflicted losses on the company. However, the point is how to turn that accumulation of personal experience into dynamic action and transform such an employee into a fighting force for the company.

No. 63 ON-SHI

World Problems Develop
from Small Matters

MINOR MATTERS SHOULD NOT BE DISREGARDED simply because they are minor; they should be considered as the beginning of major matters. Do not neglect it because it is little — rather, prudently think that it has just begun to grow larger. If problems are addressed before they become serious, they will not grow. Similarly, when someone is faced with resentment in human relations, there is no need for confrontation if one's virtues are employed to deal with it.

There is hardly anything in the world that suddenly causes huge problems or obstacles.

There is a natural process of how a huge problem or obstacle grows. First, a problem that seems like the cause appears, then it slowly starts to grow bigger or become more numerous, and finally turns into a major problem or obstacle. However, there is a way to organize a company that does not encourage the nurturing of major problems or obstacles. The problem must be eliminated when it is still in its initial stage.

Commonly, from the beginning to its end, a company's activities are devoted to work on obstacles, conflicts, or competition. The total energy of such a company has a fixed limit. So, having just begun the company, if the majority of its energy is consumed by the struggle to eliminate deficits, it might never find itself in credit, and before long it will face decline, bankruptcy, and closure — without a chance to recover.

For such companies, an important managerial issue is how to constructively employ the energy that the company possesses and how to maintain the environment attained. Utilizing its energy in such a constructive way will also help prevent the occurrence of negative issues within the company. The most appropriate and tangible means for doing this is to completely terminate the problem while it is small, minor, or easy, and this is the basic duty of business.

Yet, what can be seen at many companies is that the problem is underestimated, or may often be overlooked entirely. In others, an attitude prevails where the problem is made light of or dismissed for being too simple or easy, and thus unworthy of attention.

Major problems and obstacles do not suddenly appear without warning. Enterprises that are able to invest all of their energy constructively respect "simple honesty," which means to regard minor problems prudently and to take small matters seriously. Such enterprises, whose basic principles create an atmosphere where every employee uses his or her spiritual energy in conjunction with their duties, are able to maintain high efficiency in smoothly accomplishing major work.

Human relationships form the basis of a company's activities. The relationship between the company and customers, between the company and suppliers, between the company and trading channels, between the company and shareholders, between the company and the supervising organ of the government, between the company's executives, colleagues, and departments — no matter which one relationship is considered to be focal, they are all human relationships. Therefore, it is proper to say that a company engaging in the smooth advancement of human relationships has a distinct advantage.

How should the human relationships best be handled? It is said: "Consider your virtues and reward those who think ill of you."

A relationship between two people where one of them is thinking ill of the other may be truly called the worst relationship. However, if the person who is hated shifts and moves to share the outlook of the other and tries to understand the situation from the other's point of view, that person may stop thinking ill, and before long a sound human relationship may be built. Ill thinking, hatred, and the like, are troublesome matters that can be mitigated and completely relieved. Thus, if you exercise your virtues and consider matters from the perspective of others, it is not impossible to build a good and fruitful relationship.

No. 64 SHU-BI

Natural Forces and Cooperative Work in Top-Level Management

ONE WHO GIVES CHARITY ARTIFICIALLY spoils the deed. One who clings to something loses it. Things are promoted best when they are done naturally and unintentionally.

When one undertakes something, mistakes are most often made when the job is near completion. Take as much care at the end of the work as at the beginning. In other words, there will be no mistakes if duties are not skipped at the final packing stage, and the job is completed with the same vigor as when it was started.

The higher the level of corporate work, the more one must work in collaboration with natural forces. It resembles violin players who perform as if draining energy from outer space and pouring it into their instruments — such impressive performance does not seem due to human skill but is more of a mystery.

All things have a beginning, they grow, mature, and before long they wither. This is the law of nature. What force is behind the process when the weeds over there sprout, grow tall, make leaves and grow thickly, then before long wither and rot? This is the very power of nature.

Everything in this world is created by natural forces. Nature does not need help in order to make things grow. Yet, if the intrinsic power of nature is disregarded and replaced with too much artificial power, this actually diminishes natural powers, resulting in the loss of smooth progress and damage to the body of that object.

Superb results can be achieved if the business affairs of a company are conducted through studying and applying such natural power. When applied skillfully, this natural power of growth that everything has is also highly efficient as an energy source.

Company employees grow to be excellent professionals. By starting to work through incorporating this natural process, the company is transformed into "a mature enterprise," reflected in its relaxed and contented atmosphere, and the activities of the company become the expression of its heart.

On scrutinizing a company's activities from ongoing projects to daily business duties, most of the causes of failure are usually found in the last step of the process. A research and development project could be a typical example. In many instances of the development of a new commodity, if the boundary of the impossible is crossed and something the world formerly considered to be impossible becomes a possibility, there will be a result. Success or failure is determined at the last step of the process. Even though with just one more step, with a little more persistence, the breakthrough might appear, it is abandoned at the very last moment. With 99 percent of the job done, the final tiny step was left undone, and everything was lost — such cases abound.

"Prudence to the end" is the attitude that requires giving the same degree of attention to detail, prudence, and zeal to the concluding phases of the work as at the beginning. Suddenly the top of the mountain appears. If we recall times where we have gone through hardships, they were times when we rigorously persevered. Words of self-satisfaction may be well deserved, however, the whole complex of attention, energy, and focus that was established and made firm through the process is felt, and strength is drawn from the whole body. There are also all too frequent cases when, with only a few meters to reach the top, which is now just ahead, people are regrettably forced to turn back. Until one's foot is on the top, until the goal is reached, it is vital to think that there is still half way to go.

No. 65 JUN-TOKU

Dealing with Knowledge
in the Age of Knowledge

PEOPLE POSSESS SIMPLE MINDS AND DEEDS, and this forms the basis of the way they are. Thus, when a person tries to squelch or suppress another by showing off their knowledge, or if a person tries to rule an organization by brandishing his or her knowledge, this will instead damage the organization. This is because such use of knowledge is the source of desires and ambitions. It promotes a calculating lifestyle and tends to turn the organization into an ugly inhumane structure.

However, knowledge should also be given due importance as a resource that ought to be at the center of future business management. The time has come when technologies, know-how, and the accumulation of experience, i.e., knowledge, intellectual assets, practice, and wisdom will shape corporate strength.

Apart from its genuine value, knowledge is also a substance that is often easily misunderstood and misused. The greatest misunderstanding is the attitude that appears when someone has simply acquired up-to-date information from abroad faster than the next person, and uses the power of knowledge, brandishing it in order to gain advantage. Regarding the desire to obtain the latest information, we need to thoroughly understand the mistake of taking advantage of this because especially at the turning point, anyone can possess it.

The second misunderstanding is equating information with knowledge. True knowledge is gained not through information alone but through experience. Further, from personal experience wisdom is drawn and can be accumulated. Therefore, without practice there is no true knowledge, and without personally accumulated experience it is not possible to achieve true intellectual assets. Another good way to explain the same topic is by the realization that unless there is a balance between one's body and one's mind, there will be no human strength.

Business management is no exception to the rule that practical experience is accumulated through physical experience. Starting with mental works and through mental sharpness an "intellectual vitality" is born. It is this very accumulation that will be the strength of twenty-first-century enterprises.

Yet, inside the workings of the mind there is also strategic thought, or in other words activity going on of creatively imagining the mental picture of winning. That, too, often causes ambitions and desires. When victory or strategies for achieving victory fill the head, they are fertile soil for delusion and invention. The fresher the ideas the more intoxicated the person gets. Such a person has put all his or her energy into it and so he or she could potentially deceive a great number of people.

Once the climate of the company is violated in such a fashion, many employees could come to hate the steady way of gaining simple physical experience. They may come to prefer such mental play, and soon enough that would invite social isolation and internal distraction, the tragedy of group delusion.

Honey-tongued speeches and idle activities that are groundless and/or not related to the company's principles create a trend that lends support to idealists within the company. People who have only ideas — because they are people who only have ambitions and desires — lay the foundations for antagonism and denouncement in the company, and finally antagonism in the company arises. Self-centered conduct spreads when people decide which company clique to belong to. Such a company cannot easily maintain its business performance and it is just a matter of time before it will face decline and eventual collapse.

I believe that these are the most important points for a company's management to be aware of in this age of knowledge.

No. 66 KOH-KI

The Top Managers
of the Twenty-first Century

A TRUE LEADER HUMBLES HIMSELF OR HERSELF when she or he realizes that one stands above others. When such a person realizes that this is the case, he or she stands back and makes way for them. Governing by demonstrating power and exerting pressure is not true leadership. Rather, true leadership creates an environment where people are able to happily devote themselves to their duties and improve the results of their work.

Why does business management need leadership? Business management leadership is for the purpose of stressing organizational strength, fulfilling the company's social duties, steadily achieving goals, and for sustaining such ongoing development and completion.

Yet, there are plenty of businesses where, due to their leadership, neither the highest abilities of the employees nor the organizational strength of the business are fully demonstrated. They do not carry out their social duties or achieve their goals, and are in a permanent state of crisis.

Leaders of such businesses usually say: "In such risky situations, I am the only one capable of managing the business." In fact, it is exactly the opposite. A leader of this type should realize that he or she created that dangerous situation. Such a leader would surely refute this accusation.

So, how about the following questions? Who is supposed to be the most respected person in a business? Who comprises the business? Obviously — the clients.

Accordingly, the absolute existence of a business depends entirely upon how much it, i.e., its entire staff, respects its customers. This is simple logic. However, there are many companies' employees who think a great deal more of reaching the "top" than they do of the customers.

Many companies that theoretically work to the motto, "Customers are all important," actually run their businesses on, "The top is all important." For the regular employee it is more important how "the top" assesses him or her than how the customer does. Satisfaction of the top will have a stronger influence on the employee's circumstances than that of the customer.

Make a good inspection of the situation inside the company. Which is greater — the time spent by employees on customers, or the time spent on "the top"? Or else, what is the emphasis on? Is there a lot of work done for "the top" or preparation of materials done for internal superiors? Are these activities improving results? If this is the case, the pressure from "the top" will grow even stronger, and work done for "the top" will increase.

The correct attitude for a business is one that places emphasis on its "front," as the initial basis for setting up that business is upon customer support and customer sympathy. Which employees are the most directly and personally engaged with the customers? The president? Not very likely. Typically, the president is the least engaged with customers. It is the various persons-in-charge, namely, the "front staff."

These front staff in particular are the ones who demonstrate to the individual customer the abilities and energy of the business, the organization, and the enterprise. Thus, the era of the pyramidal organization, where "the top" reigns supreme, is over.

The role of top management is to gauge where to establish their own position of bringing up the rear, how to best deploy the front staff out to the front-line, as well as how much and what kind of support they should provide them with. The closer to front staff the emphasis is placed by a business, the more the customer is emphasized, and the greater will be the support and sympathy received from them. This will allow the business to realize its goals and continue in its development. Top management will therefore attain splendid results as well as gain increasing respect.

No. 67 SAN-POH

The Three Jewels
of Company Management

IN THE FUNDAMENTAL TEACHINGS OF THE TAO, there are three jewels. The first is tenderness. Courage also flows from a tender, loving heart. The second jewel is thrift, and this makes charity towards others possible. The third jewel is refrain — trying not to stand out ahead of others and conducting one's self modestly. This is the way that will encourage other people to follow.

The same principles also apply to business management. First, the affectionate heart; if managers have such hearts they can feel a deep affection for their employees and try to treat them with true fondness. What is true fondness? It is not pampering, but firmly guiding and nurturing them into becoming professional business men and women able to act independently, as well as providing them with the support to develop their characters and become promising people. An employee who has an affectionate heart will consider from its depths a better life and better job for the customer — their greatest delight is seeing a satisfied customer.

The affectionate heart is capable of acting selflessly. Courage flows from it just like from a mother's heart when she protects her own child. The courage that shows as the selfless actions of an affectionate heart also provides incomparable strength that will protect the concept of a business and the employees as well as assure the company's function. Thus, courage can prove the meaningful existence of an enterprise as it is the source of organizational strength that finds ways through obstacles and impediments.

Thrift is also an indispensable element of business activities. The world materialized thanks to harmony as it is comprised of "if it grows it will be cut back, if it is cut back it will grow" types of relationships. As the scope of a business's activities widens, then those kinds of relationships will necessarily increase. In determining whether something should be cut back, if there is no economy because one is indispensable, then no harmony can be achieved, and either expansion will not happen or an area one does not wish to see cut back will be cut regardless. Thus, cutting back should be made by consent. Thrift, in other words, is the secret for achieving the smooth expansion of business.

Economy has many facets, the most significant among them being the economy of energy. The need to conserve energy in an enterprise applies not only to the resources of labor, materials, and capital — it is also applicable to the resources of time and information. Economy of information involves clarifying what denotes accurate and important information, and utilizing this in the discernment of data used in order to prevent overload as well as to optimize the time available. Especially in this day of information overload, it is very important to create a system for action based on a small amount of carefully discerned information.

Don't try to take the lead from other people. The importance of modesty has been previously and repeatedly expressed. The harder a person tries to move ahead of the rest, the harder it is for him or her to achieve it. To stand clear ahead of other people is not possible without the support and recommendation from those one follows — and this should be fully comprehended.

These three principles of "affection, thrift, and refrain" are the three jewels that must neither be neglected nor forgotten by an enterprise.

No. 68 HAI-TEN

The Global Research Institute

A FIRST-RATE MILITARY COMMANDER is not ferocious. A skillful soldier does not rely on emotions or become angry. A real victory does not require rivalry with a competitor. This is known as "noncompetitive virtue."

It must be strongly emphasized that an environment of fighting is a poor one. If someone is forced to fight and fights against his or her will, the victory, if won, will have no meaning for this person.

The key to good business conduct lies in knowing how to get through without fighting — an environment without rivalry is a valuable one — as well as in knowing how to sustain that state.

A monopolistic enterprise exists when it is the only one in the world supplying its specific commodities, thus any demand for them can only be satisfied through it. In spite of the vastness of the world market, if the commodity is available solely from this enterprise there can be no competitors. The market is an "individual market" created by the same enterprise, and there is no competition at all.

The rapid expansion of the Internet is making the world seem smaller, and the more this is, the wider the commodity's distribution circle grows, making it accessible in virtually every nook and corner of the world. The global-scale monopolistic enterprise will benefit most in such an environment.

The basis of the company's unique nature is its one-of-a-kind product and its worldwide monopoly in its creation and sale. In order to create its unique product, the company possesses the "individual technology and know-how" required.

Given the lack of competition, a monopolistic enterprise has no competitive costs such as sales expenses, discounting, or advertising. Instead, these savings can be invested in the strengthening and advancement of the requisite specific technology and know-how. In this way, its degree of uniqueness increases and the company's internal condition of "good circulation" and "plus loop" continues.

With the strengthening and improving of the individual company's technology and know-how, the company's information networking — now on a global scale — can be more fully utilized and a "global brain" is mobilized. This worldwide global information network may sometimes act as a sales network, an information pool, an information provider, and sometimes a shareholders' network, etc. Any enterprise that can effectively build such a network with multiple and complex functions and establish this form of management know-how will go on to gain great strength.

Since the main features of a unique worldwide enterprise include the accumulation of management know-how of multifunctional complex networking, they will also provide a wholly advantageous base for strengthening and improving individually possessed technology and know-how. The global brain is used to network talented people scattered worldwide who have knowledge related to the com-

global
(worldwide

TAO Management

pany's technology and know-how, thus creating a kind of "global research institute."

This think tank works nonstop exchanging information and discussing common issues, the results soar and are soon integrated into new technologies and know-how that are gathered by the company. Such intellectual developments and achievements will be legally protected by the provisions of intellectual property rights laws. Then, the next assignment is approached.

So, we must respect the individual abilities of each person's mind and not neglect its restless strength for discovery. The basics of this management approach are to trust one's intuition and not to lose one's temper.

No. 69 GEN-YOH

What to Do When Noncompetitiveness Won't Work

"NONCOMPETITIVE WORLD OF HUMILITY" means living one's daily life with a noncompetitive, humble spirit, and it was the corner stone of Lao-tzu's teachings. However, what should be done if a fight is unavoidable? By no means should you take the initiative for the fight, nor make even one stride in your foe's direction. You wait prudently and make your next move depending on your foe's behavior. Should your foe come near, step back in order to maintain distance between you. Then if your foe continues to attack, you have given the foe nothing to grasp nor any means to fight.

There are times in business when a competitive situation is forced upon you and it is unavoidable. What is the best thing to do in such situations? First, during battle, you must think yourself "undefeatable." Next, you must think of victory. In order not to lose, the enemy should not be underestimated.

Not to underestimate means not to engage in the battle thoughtlessly. When, even though one has no will for fighting but still the fight breaks out, it means that the foe is underestimating the opposition. Thus, the foe already adds the element of defeat to his or her plan of attack.

When one is underestimated by one's foe it means that the foe is thoroughly prepared to attack the point that he or she despises.

When it comes to the fight, the customers that have a connection to the foe should first be cared for as standard politeness should not be forgotten. By doing this, the foe's hostility will diminish and his or her fighting strength will decrease considerably.

At the same time, the rival will loosen his or her grip on the initiative to engage in a fight and may avoid further advances. If the foe does come near, one simply steps back in order to maintain distance. Not to react predictably to the foe's plan is to knock him or her off balance, deprive him or her of reading one's intentions, share no information, and thus effectively counter the next attack.

Further, keeping a fixed distance between oneself and one's foe creates a regular buffer zone. This discourages attacks and allows one to keep a watch on one's rival. If an attack follows, any means for protection might be considered, yet simply watching may often serve to dishearten the foe and when repeated, wear him or her out. Though the foes try to attack, they cannot; though they try to engage in combat they cannot; and though they try to knock one down, they fail.

When such circumstances continue, mistrust towards the leader of the foe's camp grows. Since they have not made progress as planned, the leader's appropriateness for command as well as his or her strategy-building ability is questioned, as is that leader's command as a whole.

In the meantime, the fighting morale at the foe's camp drops. Hostility no longer prevails since hatred and anguish are no longer gushing out. Ultimately, the foe simply loses his or her stamina, can no longer sustain the desire to fight, and the hostility thus ends. Responsibility is subsequently sought, typically leading to the loss of many talented people from the foe's camp. Further still, the psychological aftereffects resulting from the battle-inflicted losses remain and may constitute a considerable weakness for the former rival.

Eventually, the company's way of handling animosity will become widely known in society, with the result that from then on no company will willingly take the chance of demonstrating hostility towards it. Increasingly, then, the condition of "victory without fighting" will be created.

No. 70 CHI-NAN

What Is a Mature Company?

ALTHOUGH THE TAO TEACHINGS OF LAO-TZU are essentially easy to comprehend and carry out, Taoism does not flagrantly promote itself when offering its truths, thus very few people actually study, understand, and practice the Tao. Given an absence of practical profit hunting and lack of direct tangible results in the discipline as taught, interest in learning and following the Tao is generally low and its spread has been restricted. Nevertheless, it is said that this is exactly what validates its teachings.

An enterprise is an entity that matures while progressing. What does maturing mean in this case? There is the maturing of an enterprise's function as a contributor to society. Is the enterprise contributing and helping to create a more dignified life with regard to that most fundamental of problems in human life — disease? Is the enterprise providing enough support for this?

From a different viewpoint, what contribution to "safety, peace of mind, and security" is the enterprise making to people's lives? Safety is a measure of progress in protecting humankind from disasters, including natural and human-made calamities. Is the enterprise contributing to this? Peace of mind is a measure of the kind and extent of support that exists for people in times of turmoil during disasters. It is a measure of every aspect of the system for protection of human lives including the availability of systems, goods, and services. Is the enterprise sufficiently performing a supporting role for these activities? Security is a measure of support such as products and services for systems covering loss of income through disability. Are there enough of these formulated?

It is necessary for enterprises to tackle the above problems with more passion as well as on a broader front, and to revise their attitudes so as not to deprive people of their safety, peace of mind, and security in times of disaster. Next, is the enterprise maturing as a human group while it progresses? Does it succeed in being a suitable place for each person to spend her or his uniquely valuable lifetime?

There is a need to examine whether the chance for each individual to lead an independent life is sufficiently given. Or, on the contrary, is it becoming a place where opportunities are nipped in the bud, human nature is scarred, and there are more harmful effects inflicted than good?

Concurrently, is the enterprise becoming a place where a range of valuable experiences can be tasted as well as being a place of new self-discovery? In this light, it is of value to compare the enterprise as a whole with an orchestra, or a film-production team, or with a professional sports team like baseball or soccer, or any other group of professionals, and to appraise the extent of its improvement on such a basis. Then, are the company employees and managers equally maturing in their fields as do famous painters, craftsmen, Japanese chess or *go* players who continually strive to improve their individual level of skill and excellence?

Through the consideration of these things, we can clearly understand that the Tao teachings of Lao-tzu offer a model well worth emulating in the pursuit of excellence and maturity as business professionals, for employees and managers alike. This strongly suggests that the secret of maturity for the business of tomorrow lies within Tao Management.

No. 71 CHI-HEI

A Company with No End

DO NOT PARADE YOUR KNOWLEDGE when you know something. It is wrong to feign knowledge of something when you do not know. The Tao teachings have immeasurable depth; they are not something that is easily exhaustible. The more one knows the more unknowns appear, and it is impossible to feign knowledge of these. Thus, the more one is aware of one's own blind spots and knows that she or he still has a lot to understand, the more possible it becomes to address and eliminate them.

There is no such thing as an end to a business. In other words, not using continuity to one's advantage means that one cannot use fate advantageously. The advantage of utilizing continuity well is that the pressures of deadlines then cease and thus there is always time for challenge.

If goals are gradually set higher, one can climb to heights beyond all expectations. Even a slow pace is fine, as sudden upturns followed by abrupt downturns are unfavorable for business. It is best to climb to the top with small but steady paces. In this way, the importance of "improvement" as a goal or condition for a business becomes clear.

knowledge - attain
technology - possess

However, the question here is whether there exists such a high goal worthy of being challenged continually over the long term. Just as when people of ancient times laid the foundations of the giant castle walls, they knew that it would not be completed in their generation. What is a great and broad purpose that may be built upon ceaselessly for three, four, or more generations?

The answer that emerges is a high, eminently suitable goal that is not easily achievable. This is the pursuit of the Tao that is the eternal truth.

What managers and employees should pay close attention to here is "knowing their weaknesses." What is required for improvement? First, it is the ability to discern clearly what one knows, what one can do, what one does not yet know, and what one cannot yet do. Therefore, the spreading trend of pretending to know what is still unknown to one and pretending to be able to do things that one cannot do actually impedes improvement.

By turning modestly to him or herself and studying his or her own nature each employee can precisely determine the answers to the following queries: What do I still not know? What are the drawbacks in my character that I still haven't attended to? Where are my blind spots or weaknesses that make my skills insufficient? Then, the lack of knowledge, drawbacks, blind spots, and the weaknesses that have been determined must be tackled. As they are remedied, this exercise should be repeated. There is nothing that can more accurately help improve an individual's abilities than this.

On an organizational level as well, one must determine what knowledge must be attained and what technology should be possessed, and then one must address doing so. The traditional custom of carrying out business in fixed time periods is one of a few methods that activates and favorably turns the fate of the eternal enterprise.

This world is preserved through its balance. Given this, then one needs to firmly establish one's worthy points in order to counter or offset the many drawbacks and weak points one possesses. What is a "worthy point"? It is, "Something you know to suffice." Do not forget to be grateful for the present state of affairs, for the fact that you are living, and for the job you are doing today. Put simply, do not complain. Rather, be satisfied.

Liking the Job, Liking the Boss, Liking the Company

IT IS SAID that there will always be severe divine punishment when people do not fear God or are conceited. Lao-tzu did not use any religious expressions to inspire fear. He simply stated: Do not despise your place even if it is tiny and do not hate your occupation. Those people who do not disgust will not incur Heaven's disgust.

The earth we live on had its beginning together with Heaven. Heaven and earth are one. Therefore, the condition of Heaven will also be the condition of earth for there is nothing between them. What Heaven dislikes people also dislike and what people dislike Heaven also dislikes. Likewise, as business is a part of this system, then these structures would also be reflected in the organization — this is the key.

Further, if a great number of a company's employees hate their job, hate their superiors, and hate their company, then that will also be hated by Heaven. Managers urgently need to consider the radical and drastic implications of this.

Why do they hate their job, their superiors, and/or their company? What should be done in order to make them like it?

What will happen if you force someone who hates to like? How do you make people really like something?

Let's begin with the "company's intention" — the sympathetic response to the company's vision. Initially, there is an inner ring of sympathetic response to the aspirations of the company and the business is formed in order to respond to this.

Whatever the job, everybody wants to do the work they aspire to. No matter what their income, everyone wants to earn the amount they wish.

I would like to take a look at the situation where demands are often made for personal desires and personal likes to meet the aspirations of the company. While it is necessary that both parties take steps towards each other, there is no need for compromise because the product of compromise eventually becomes unreasonable and it does not last long. There is no need for unreasonableness. If no common ground is sought, it should be considered a happy outcome for both parties. This provides the perfect opportunity for the company to sincerely choose the most suitable employee and vice versa for employees, to choose the company that satisfies them.

If its aspirations are unclear, then the company must reexamine its societal role. When the company's social duties are reexamined, none are to be drawn from its past. Far better to imagine that "the company starts from tomorrow" and to consider what social obligations should be undertaken and then in what way to structure the company.

Thus, having established common ground based upon their intentions, the next step should be to offer the following questions to each employee: "Why it is not boring to play mahjong through the night, yet it is to work?" The an-

swer is prompt: "Because I don't find the job interesting!"
"But why isn't the job interesting?"

In order to receive a relevant response to this question, one prior question must be asked. "So, was mahjong interesting right from the very beginning?"

Most likely, then the rules were not well understood, nor what constitutes a winning hand. At this time was it really so enthralling? No doubt, it was not so interesting at all. Whatever it may be, the more interesting something grows to be later on, the less interesting it was at the start.

"So, when did it become interesting?" After winning. Even one experience of victory is enough — it will become the source of motivation.

How was it won? It was won because the person "achieved the necessary level of abilities." Therefore, in order to feel the thrill of what one is doing, it is necessary to first acquire a minimum amount of skill. This may also be called "the level of ability for feeling interested." The key point here is how to train people to achieve this standard of ability.

No. 73 NIN-I

Making Use of Natural Powers

THE TAO DOES NOT OPPOSE ANYTHING, but it defeats everything. The Tao does not say anything but pays the villain with atrocity and the good with favors. Occasionally, there are times when the good cannot make it through and the villain triumphs. However, if we look over the long term, disaster strikes those who violate the Tao and good fortune comes to those who follow. Heaven does not set anyone free from its net — we are all enmeshed.

Corporate management ought to consider making increased use of "natural ethics." Businesses that are engaged in inappropriate affairs or cause suffering to their employees violate the principles of the Tao. Therefore, they will eventually end up in disgrace — even though it may be a slow process — and they will not be able to sustain full development.

Yet in the real world, businesses or managers that hardly seem to be conforming to the Tao are running their affairs amazingly successfully; nourished and prosperous, they pride themselves on being in the prime of life. Temporarily, it certainly happens. However, it is by no means a viable, long-term prospect.

As expected, the teachings of the Tao will persevere. Then the villain will perish but the good will prevail. Heaven's net is of tremendous size and so people have a tendency to think that there are perhaps one or two human exceptions to the teachings. But the Tao never lets anything slip through the net. There are no exceptions. You, me, we are all caught. The Tao, or Heaven, or nature all work in such a way.

To be a winner without competing is the way nature works. Since there are no battles, there is no occasion for contests. Consequently, if there are no contests there can be no victors. Yet it would be erroneous to think it impossible to become a winner. Winning means to snatch the booty forcefully from the enemy — this is inconsistent with, and opposes, the Taoist teachings that say such conduct is against the action of nature. It is impossible to keep on winning forever. Defeat will eventually come.

Or rather, perhaps the opponent is revived. One is now living with the enemy. How about if enterprises presently in competition instead cooperate among themselves to expand on a global scale? Some things that may be impossible for one company to do could be realized by two or more. Therefore, the fact that your competitor lives means that you also live.

What if you exercise your courage not on competing but on cooperating with the competitor enterprise? Doing so is suited to the way nature works, and thus it becomes possible to win and receive support from the power of nature. Further, since following the Tao allows you to receive such support, why not gather together followers of the Tao and those possessing analogous qualities — and run the company with them as employees or clients or customers?

Expand the circle of people who work following the Tao and form a global network for sympathizers and those who accept its basic ideas. How about extending support regardless of differences in geography and race to all followers living by the Tao?

If everybody — naturally including the employees, and from the suppliers and cooperative companies, to the customers, clients, and shareholders — is a follower of the Tao, an enormous natural strength would be attained. An enterprise whose management operates with ready access to such a vast natural resource will never perish.

※ 企業 — 滅ばない

No. 74 SEI-WAKU

Joyful and Grateful Management

THE ACTIONS OF NATURE IN THE WORLD, i.e., the work of the Tao, do not overlook an unreasonable person. The law of God always chastises the villain and supports the good one. Accordingly, a person who tries to rule in place of God by punishing people is like using a dull, rusty saw instead of using the fine tool of an excellent carpenter — that person will be unable to avoid hurting himself or herself. Therefore, administrators must exercise the authority to punish very carefully.

The time when businesses could be run based upon punishment and fear is over. Rather, the next generation of businesses will be run based on desire, pleasure, and the creation of stable, enjoyable, and fulfilling lives.

The best treatment for an incurable disease like cancer is "delight and pleasure." Thanks to delight and pleasure the natural healing power, the ability to resist illnesses, and the functions of the immune system of the human body are strengthened. In this attitude of "delight and gratitude" thus lies the strength that is the source of the power of life. On the contrary, in "anger, fear, and sorrow" is hidden the source of illness.

What type of enterprise would run itself by the rule of fear, inviting indignation for its cruel human relations and resultant grief of scared people? It would not be an exaggeration to say that social contributions express regret for social evil. This is the complete opposite of being the "reason for existing," as typically stated by businesses.

Enterprises must become social sources of "delight and gratitude" in order to establish then demonstrate their meaningful existence. An enterprise that consists of sick employees cannot offer high quality goods and services. "Well, then what is the proper way to treat a bad employee or person?" One must consider what is the best Tao approach. The ultimate job for managers is to consider the best way to enliven their employees.

Who will enforce the punishment? This should be left to Providence. It is best to entrust it to the Tao and Heaven. Why? Because nature has the power to rob all things of life.

Why does nature's Providence possess such actions? Because no one but Providence can fulfill such an extremely difficult job. It is simply not a job that — compared with the Tao and Heaven — a thoughtless and stupid human can do. If a person should be entrusted with this, just as if one hammers a knife instead of a great smith or handles a sharp knife instead of an acclaimed chef — it would be more surprising were one not to be cut. Exercising penal regulations instead of Heaven must be carried out with due humility and an extremely cautious spirit. Some people may enjoy a pleasant feeling from the manipulation of their own thoughts as they instill fear in others through punishment. We must be mindful and wary of such feelings.

The person who is ruining order in an enterprise naturally becomes obvious. What should be done if this happens? Of course, one must be fair. One must give guidance. One must be mindful.

In order to give this guidance fairly, managers need to put all of their efforts towards turning the enterprise into a living body of "delight and gratitude." Although all employees may be working towards the realization of such desirable and splendid goals, if then there is a troublemaker, he or she will be showered with criticism from all the other employees and forced to change before the manager needs to mete out punishment.

No. 75 DON-SON

The Adhering Partner Is Different

AT FIRST GLANCE, heavy taxation duties may appear to be imposed for the good of the country. However, if this causes citizens to become desperate and implement such drastic action as taking their own lives, then ultimately taxes cannot be satisfactorily collected and the country will grow weak. Exactly in the same way, if executives implement too many measures driven by their own interests, the result will be the opposite of what they expect — the executives will take losses. One might ask, "Why will there be too many measures?" The answer is because of excessive regard for one's own circumstances and way of thinking.

A business is run with the utmost aim of achieving "sustained, full expansion." Whatever happens, the continuation of the business must be ensured and temporary closure or bankruptcy excluded. However, if too much emphasis is placed on the continuation of the business and this one point is disproportionally clung to, it could instead shorten the life of the company.

Another problem with placing excessive emphasis on the full continuation of the business is that then too much attention is paid to making profits. Profit is the value added by the company. Therefore, if increased profit is desired, all efforts should first be put into the creation of added value. How can the company offer products of even more fantastic value? Focusing on this, the main topic that will surface and need to be dealt with is: "What does the customer consider to be value?"

Yet, what happens if one thinks too much about the profits? Definitely, the ability to offer and create added value would improve; however, efforts would be solely focused upon increasing profit-taking calculations. As a result, overbearing trading methods could not be avoided. The company would be forced into pressure sales and selling through intimidation.

When the full continuation of the business is overemphasized, the excess attachment to turnover would instead threaten the company's own well-being. The sales volume growth requirements coerce employees into increasing their sales by just one more no matter what it takes. The more pressure the managers put on them, the more overbearing the sales practices they use, and these are beyond the control of the company.

Turnover means the value retrieved from the buyer in return for the value offered by the company. Business means the exchange of value between buyers and sellers. In other words, unless one offers high value, the other will not return high value, i.e., she or he will not pay high charges. Offering unique value that cannot be found anywhere else brings buyers to the company doors begging, "Please sell me one," and eradicates the need for sales.

Marketing means value creation. In effect it does away with sales. However, if one is only concerned with turnover, all attention focuses on how to increase the sales volume, and this leads to completely ignoring the provision of value. In this way the company lets slip its creation as well as provision of value, and its vitality suffers.

Consequently, business managers must never lose sight of the fundamentals. Nor can the company afford to forget its essential social obligations. It must put them right at the core of the company and refer to them diligently.

# No. 76 KAI-KYOH

Management Where Flexibility Is Vital

A HUMAN HAS A SOFT AND WEAK BODY at birth and a stiff body at death. Similarly, grass and trees are soft when they grow and hard when they wither. Trees like the oak tree, which are rigid and strong, can be snapped by storms that soft trees like the willow can endure. While notions like soft and weak represent life, rigidity and strength represent death.

The initiation of management that knows the importance of flexibility has begun. To date, the typical company has, if anything, been strengthened to resemble an unsinkable battleship. From development and production to sales and after-service, or from materials and products to accessories production, the goal was for all items to be completed and supplied by the company itself. Further, the ideal scenario was that the entire process would be done by the company's employees.

This approach resulted in the creation of entities that were disciplined in large-scale in-house perfectionism. Such companies were thought to be the best and thus ones to be proud of. However, such enterprises lacked flexibility and suffered because they could not respond to sudden changes in technological innovation or shifting market conditions. Now companies must do a 180-degree turn and introduce management that can be more flexible.

What should be done? To be soft means to possess no shape. It means not being selfishly insistent. Similarly, the organization also exists on the condition that it adapts according to circumstances and can make a multiplicity of changes.

Just as a baseball team's coach determines the batting order having predicted the competing team's pitchers for that day, the head of the workplace must likewise compose a team according to the task at hand. Prior to the team's formation, the various assignments of those who will be nominated as its members function as a waiting room or a holding pattern.

Naturally, there will be those who are frequently nominated and those who aren't. For those who aren't, as in professional baseball, where players are dropped into the minor leagues for retraining, similarly employees are sent for additional training to strengthen and supplement their basic skills.

In significant contrast to the baseball team, however, the working team can take on outside professionals at any time. The working team can thus make use of external human resources, and would be well advised to make maximum use of this advantage. A very important duty of any personnel division is to have good information on the whereabouts of highly skilled human resources and their present assignments. This is external resource administration.

Teams composed by joining external and internal resources — in other words a team that brings together precisely the right skills for the assignment — then form the structure of that enterprise. The job of the organizational administration, or "Knowledge-link Producer" is to discover how to draw the best from the mixed team, as well as how to allow them to demonstrate all of their abilities in order to further enhance their efficacy and thus attain high quality results. The Knowledge-link Producer is expected to carefully screen each team member's individual abilities, personality, etc., and discover how best to ignite her or his creativity and intellectual processes — the key resources of a working group — in order to produce results beyond expectations.

Since the structure of the enterprise is always temporary, the design of the office will naturally have to change as well. Fixed desks and chairs are not suitable. Each person should be assigned her or his own cabinet, set on castors, so the cabinet can be moved freely to wherever the employee will sit that day. Every space in the office should be available. One can then sit down to work wherever one feels comfortable. This encourages flexibility of thought. Communication between company employees should be conducted through email and conversations via cellular phones and laptop personal computers.

How thoroughly flexibility is investigated, encouraged, and incorporated will become the deciding factor for the enterprise's growth.

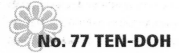

No. 77 TEN-DOH

Corporate Strength Is Born
of Harmony

TAO RESPECTS HARMONY, suppresses higher people, and supports lower ones. It reduces those who have and gives to those who have not. People behave in exactly the opposite way; they further reduce the possessions of the have-nots who are already suffering through their insufficiencies, and the haves take it all. While doing great work the Tao does not try to rely on its successes or demonstrate its power, and that is how it rules over everything.

What is the right way to continually and smoothly demonstrate the total power that makes up the enterprise's strength? First, one needs to define what corporate strength actually is.

A sphere is the ideal form for an enterprise. The necessary condition for this is to be evenly formed — neither imbalances in any managerial functions or resources, nor in the discrimination of weak or strong points. Corporate strength is that which is demonstrated as the entirety of its abilities. In other words, a company's entire ability encompasses its possession of technological strength, that of product development as well as its capital, and the company's image itself.

Then, what is the main factor? It is "harmony."

Rather than whether the right ability is available in one isolated area, the full range of a company's total ability is increased when each skill is evenly matched. Managers should always oversee not a part but the entire body of the enterprise and never create obscure posts or make calculations in isolation. For example, measures should be taken so that proper attention is being paid to the branch offices. All too often their needs and operations tend to be overlooked or dismissed. Further, always have a glance over the main figures from an individual or a branch in order to avoid unclear areas.

So, by properly gathering company information of a determined quantity and nature, the enterprise or company as a whole is imagined to be one sphere. Then, in order not to create future weaknesses, branches that have satisfactory skills and those that need reinforcing can be identified and a precise plan for appropriate strengthening proposed.

Yet, there is one more important point that needs consideration, namely, the cycles that affect both humans and organizations. Unavoidably, differences between favorable and unfavorable conditions do appear. This is exactly what causes distortions to the balance of the whole.

Management needs to grasp the present state of branches and people accurately. In times of recession, when certain branches or people have slumped, aid should be provided straight from the top layers of the company to make up the deficit of skill and power until performance has been brought up to the same level as that of other departments, and total company balance is reinstated.

Should a situation be created where people or departments drag upon the whole entity, the strength of the enterprise would be significantly hampered. Such a situation should be avoided at all costs, even if this means directly involving the top executives.

Management has to know the whole company inside out and provide thorough support for weakened and unbalanced departments or people. This evocation and nurturance of the entire company's potential is the prime duty of management. However, it is not good policy to venture anything about this.

Why? If you relate that, thanks to support from the top, they somehow managed to achieve their performance targets successfully, it could not help but diminish the confidence of the party that was assisted. What's more, it would also invite a reaction from other employees and departments that had persevered on their own.

Therefore, assistance provided by top-layer executives should be conducted incognito. It is hard to predict how beneficial it will be for the company if that assisted party is led to believe that they managed the job on their own and their confidence is boosted.

No. 78 NIN-SHIN

The Courage to Face Up
to All the Company's Misfortunes

THERE IS NOTHING ON EARTH as tender as water. It
flows down and downward — it can never flow up-
ward. The saint who has adopted the state of water accepts
the whole country's filth, humiliation, and adversity upon
himself or herself. People tend to think that the monarch is
the recipient of the honor and blessing of the country, but
acceptance of this downward flow is actually the way of a
true leader.

The most important duty of a company manager is to
achieve sustained, full development of his or her company during the term of office and to hand over the reins
smoothly to one's successor. The manager naturally bears
the responsibility for the company while in office, and he or
she must also bear a part of its responsibility even in the
future.

Why? The development of innovative technology takes
no less than ten years. This means that ten years prior to the
development of now innovative technology, decisions such

as how to conduct what kinds of R&D had to be made, the budget for the research had to be approved, and the research had to begin. This was so not only for technological development but also for the various preceding investment conditions.

There are surprisingly many things that, although the results will come ten, maybe twenty years later, must be started now. The success or failure of the company ten years hence can only be anticipated from the resolute step of the present-day managers. After results, there is nothing more telling of a manager's performance than whether they successfully modeled for the next generation of managers the resolve necessary to begin matters that would likely be challenging and demanding and that they would not see through to completion.

Isn't this the way managers ought to be — consenting to things that will bring them no honor or rewards and having the courage to take on tough work? If they push ahead in this way, ultimately the next generation of managers can simply implement what their predecessors planned and began, and then plan for the subsequent generation. This is a seemingly minus situation for the present that the company accepts completely.

Many events take place as a result of carrying out the company's activities. There are plenty of honors as well as social approval. However, there are also failures and humiliations. One needs the courage to deal with the filth gathered over the long run — bad social habits and infamous behavior, illegal transactions and affairs — without running for cover but facing all challenges directly, and without delaying but resolving the problems during one's own term.

Accordingly, the problem has bright and clear as well as wet and dark sides. Executives are installed as troubleshooters, to absorb the dark side and to give the bright and clear sides to their employees. Thus, people who care only to be flamboyant and stand out are not fit to be managers.

Since the true leader's ideal is for work to progress through the natural power of the organization, his or her presence is not felt — her or his ideal is to be so inconspicuous that one is not sure quite what she or he is doing. An enterprise with a leader who avoids standing out and takes full responsibility for his or her company's misfortunes, has a firm foundation and it will not flinch over minor matters. Because it doesn't flinch, such minor matters all but disappear. Villains will stay away and bad social habits will not breed. Finally, one would see excellent conditions arise and be sustained, and as a result, the manager will duly receive the honors and rewards she or he merits.

No. 79 NIN-KEI

New Management Ideas — A Universal Outlook

TRYING TO SOFTEN GREAT HOSTILITY that was once harbored is to no avail, as it will continue to remain for a long, long time. A sage, for example, does not try to collect his money relentlessly from a borrower even if he passes by. He writes a bond of debt and waits. This is because lending, not collecting the debt is the principal thing.

An era marked by new management ideas has begun. What are these new ideas?

Business management activities are conducted within the context of the universe. Therefore, shouldn't businesses stop restricting their activities to the human social context alone, widen their outlook to include the whole universe, and find significance in its philosophy?

Lao-tzu said, "A good man does not have disrespect for the teachings of Heaven." In the teachings of Heaven, there is no such thing as partiality. However, they are allies of the good person and provide them with help. What makes a good person? A good person is someone who embodies the Tao teachings.

Since humans generally want to achieve results within a brief period of time, would a good person — one who embodies the Tao — not be making permanent losses? Doesn't a bad person, competitive and strengthened by force and desire, actually make profits and enjoy a good life?

The timing of the heavenly Tao may be erratic perhaps, but it will be an ally of the good and will come to their aid. I would like you to take one more look at the so-called winner. Does he or she feel truly satisfied? Is he or she truly happy? In addition, how long will this fortune continue for the "victor"?

The management of tomorrow must embody the state of the Tao and make practical use of the actions of nature and the universe. Indeed, I strongly suggest that they introduce new management ideas based on this philosophy. This is Tao Management.

One of the main points of the Tao is "generosity and leeway." Business management can continuously extend times of "delight and gratitude" to their employees by fulfilling its social duties brilliantly.

There are three essential points. First, always take a long-term view of the company. Second, the company's social obligations should be intensified. Third, the main intention must be set without forgetting the various other concerns. Succinctly, one should not lose one's "generous" spirit. The universe is generous above all else. Although the balance of accounts can be settled at any time, it is better when it remains open. In the long run, losses will be greater if people with potential are not made the most of, if people who could be useful are lost, and if great resentment is suffered as a result.

What is the main requirement in order not to lose this "generous" mentality? Spare room to maneuver is essential. Leeway implies routinely stopping at 70 percent and reserving 30 percent. For financial administration within the company as well, investment should typically be curtailed at 70 percent and 30 percent kept as reserve. All energies should be poured into the 70 percent.

What should be done to get the most from that 70 percent? "Prediction." All serious matters and problems should be resolved before they develop further, i.e., whilst they are still easy to deal with. It takes very little effort to effectively deal with a matter if it is still small and weak. Strike while the iron is hot. Do it while there is no one around and there is no competition.

So, what is the essence of making accurate predictions? It is "freedom from avarice." This is to act without self-interest and to be purely concerned with making social contributions and being useful in society.

No. 80 DOKU-RITSU

The Ideal Company — Small Organization, Few Employees, Global-scale Intentions

LAO-TZU'S TEACHING ON UTOPIA also applies to the ideal enterprise. He states that the ideal country is a small one with only a moderate population.

The era of proud large-scale enterprises with great numbers of employees is over. It is now an era where one is proud not of a company's size, but of an essential existence in society; not of the number of employees but of the number of sympathetic respondents outside of the company walls.

Employees' energy should not be wasted on unnecessary matters. They should selflessly strive to carry out their own roles. For them, the days will then pass with a sense of fulfillment in the sustained knowledge that their own abilities are improving and with the satisfaction of being able to carry out their duties. People naturally respect death, and seek to live full lives. Let them feel at home at the company and never think of leaving it.

Employees live with the main objective of seeing their own lives bloom. If they are grateful that their own company is the best place to be as the main stage of their lives, no matter what temptations may come their way, employees will never consider transferring to another company. Even if a job has a slightly better pay and a slightly higher position, will people stay long term in a job or at a company they do not consider to be worthwhile since they only have one life to live? A good company is one that is rich in opportunities for their employees to spread their wings, respects its employees' lives, and takes care of that vitality.

The time when companies paraded their competitive strength is over. What is the purpose of high-quality goods and services? It is certainly not for competing. It is for superbly carrying out the company's role in society. No other company can fulfill all areas of this company's social role. On a global scale no other company manufactures goods like this company's goods. It is a unique enterprise. Therefore, there is no such thing as competition for this kind of company.

Return to contract conditions binding people with an ancient simple rope, that of mutual respect and honor. While civilization has provided many advantages, I feel we have also been deprived of our "real emotional interchange" and "tranquil lives." Civilization has progressed in terms of surface brilliance. However, it offers us a diminished sense of fulfillment from our good job performance. Weapons of astonishing capacity have been developed, compounding the danger in our own lives. Knowledge made humans smarter, but at the same time it also bred selfishness and inhumanity thanks to the delusion that some of us are invincible. If we consider the company to have no substitute as a place to spend one's uniquely valuable life, then perhaps the areas that should be given greatest significance are in providing "real emotional interchange" and a "tranquil life."

People know what they feel satisfied with right now. So, they can be content with where they live, what they eat, what they wear, and the environment they are in currently. An attitude of "gratitude and delight" is what must be encouraged within the company. First, be grateful about the current conditions of your life, that there are no major problems or serious concerns. Then, in order to pursue a happy life and attain satisfaction from your job, you must aim for even greater excellence in your technical skills. The more skillful, the more eminent you become, the greater the delight.

The value supplied by the company, i.e., its product and/or services, is an expression of an attitude respectful of the pursuit of gratitude and happiness. The potency of a grateful and happy heart may also be directly conveyed to the customers, reminding them of its prime importance. If this ripples out until it reaches the most distant places of the globe, its course will be reversed and waves of sympathy towards the source company will flood back. This is the way the Tao works.

**No. 81 KEN-SHITSU**

The Non-beautiful, Untalkative, Non-extensive, Non-accumulating, Noncompetitive

TRUTHFUL WORDS ARE NOT BEAUTIFULLY DECORATED. Beautifully decorated words are not words of truth. A person of truly good conduct does not play with words. A talkative person is not doing good deeds. Likewise, the face of true value is not decorated, so do not forget that it is often mistaken at first glance or overlooked.

What is righteous? What is truth? Lao-tzu gave the following answers:

- "Without beauty" — this means not being beautifully decorated.
- "Without speech" — i.e., not being talkative.
- "Without extensiveness" — not having excessive or extraneous surface knowledge.
- "Without accumulation" — means not being greedy.

- "Without competition" — never entering into competition.

A beautifully decorated object draws attention to its surface although it may contain something of great value. So the real truth of the object is hidden from view or even shunned. Further, the more thickly the surface is decorated the harder it is to see the contents. If one has confidence in the contents themselves any extra decoration is superfluous. It is far better not to make such valuable contents invisible.

The proposals of an intelligent person are excellent indeed in their skillful wording and he or she can easily exert influence. Using counter arguments, such a person can also create and present sound reasoning, make a verbal escape, or even make an illogical argument seem consistent. Being forced to use many words means that one does not know the core of the matter, and one is trying to deceive by dressing up the vague details that are known.

Extensive surface knowledge comes from grasping at shadows. People with a thirst for knowledge may know all sorts of things, but they know nothing about the true mental state. We must seek the truth and take it seriously. It does not have to be such a difficult task. This is the only teaching of the Tao.

This world is in permanent motion. Not one thing is stationary. Property and possessions are no exceptions, and restricting their movement by accumulating them in one place is unhealthy. Further, the more one gives to another person, the more one's possessions will grow and the wealthier one will become.

Why? The more one gives into circulation, the more returns. This means that things can be supplied without problem should the time come when they are necessary. When they are not needed, no amount of property or possessions will help to propel one. Instead, valuable energy is spent in their upkeep. It is enough to provide these things when they are needed. This is the meaning of true abundance.

The most flexible substance in the natural world — water — flows according to its own nature. It finds little openings and enters places it wants to enter and it can assume any form to match that of the space it fills. Thus, water does not compete with anything. Competing expresses the failure of one's intentions to progress as planned. Water has nothing to compete with since it progresses as expected. Since there is no competition, no surplus energy is wasted. That is why it is possible to invest all its energies if needed.

The time has come for businesses to establish the importance of truth and the true mental state as their ideal, and to then invest their concentrated energies in fulfilling their own role, i.e., the "non-beautiful," "untalkative," "non-extensive," "non-accumulating," "noncompetitive" ideal expounded by Lao-tzu. By so doing, businesses can bring about their own immortality.

TAO Company

Practice Section

THE BASIC STRUCTURE of a "Tao Company" — an enterprise that practices Tao Management — is comprised of the following elements.

Future Prediction is a discipline that throws light on the actual condition of space and humankind. Its teaching is revealed in the "SIX GI" (principles that recognize and acknowledge interrelationships). The Six Gi are divided into the THREE GI of cognition and the THREE GI of the law.

First, the three Gi of cognition are as follows:

SHO (image) — there are various images in the Universe, and
SUU (numbers) — all of them can be converted into numbers
RI (reason) — to understand the philosophy of the universe.

When one applies these to the company, they become:

> SHO (image) — there are various flexible activities, and
> SUU (numbers) — all of them are settled through calculations
> RI (reason) — which helps understand the meaning of their existence.

Naturally, "Heaven and Earth are united" and "Business activities" as part of Earth's activities are in agreement with Heaven.

Next, the three Gi of the law are as follows:

> HEN (change) — the law of the ever-changing Universe
> FUHEN (stability) — the law of the constant eternity
> KAN (simplicity) — in simple clarity is the core of the matter

If the above three postulations are applied to the company as the indispensable factors, we obtain:

> HEN (change) — the principle of development
> FUHEN (stability) — the principle of prosperity
> KAN (simplicity) — the principle of satisfaction

Corporate development means to thrive on the active application of "change" in era, sense of values, and the latest technologies. Further, corporate development mandates the appropriate and efficient application of the energy that derives from change. Change in turn can come about through critique and interactions by more and more of those who are sharing the same feelings about ideological assertions, forming ever-widening concentric circles.

Prosperity refers to the value of that "stability" that rides on the waves of change. Further, prosperity is created through employing the mechanism of stability.

The purpose of corporate development and the creation of prosperity is to bring satisfaction to people. In turn, their core truth is satisfaction.

The three principles are explained as follows, and of course, what is built into the total body called "company" also is closely connected to the "individuals" who work there as employees. Further activity of the firm is displayed in two elements: "human collectivism" and "strategic organization."

Drawing a diagram of the above, we obtain:

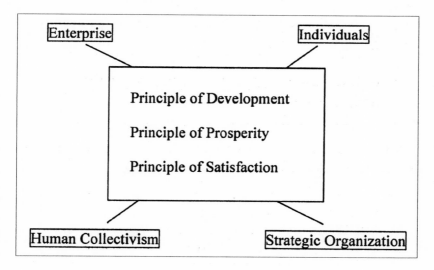

Let me explain, using the three principles.

It must be kept in mind that the three principles of "development," "prosperity," and "satisfaction" exist in ongoing relationship with each other, in stimulation of each other, and in support of each other.

- Development is impossible without prosperity and satisfaction.

- Prosperity is impossible without development and satisfaction.
- Satisfaction is impossible without prosperity and development.

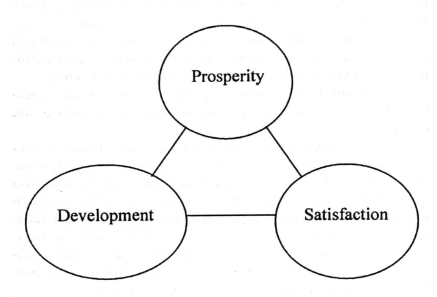

1. The Principle of Development

The main attribute of development is the absence of "stagnating, stopping, and failing." What should be done to attain this condition on a more permanent basis? "Reject rivalry and humble yourself." What does "reject rivalry" mean? For that, conditions free of "conflict" and "competition" should be attained. What does "free of conflict" mean? The absence of a conflict between "sellers and buyers." The development of commodities mandates that the views and opinions of the consumer — an amateur — be routinely incorporated with those of the manufacturing company — the professional. Such data must be gathered continuously, not only during various specific occasions.

"Various specific occasions" includes direct interviews. It can also refer to indirect exchange of opinions via questionnaires or the media. Further, such "occasions" arise simultaneously with the sales of products at the time of after-sales service, reclamation, idea collection via suggestions or comments, testing, after purchase, after usage, etc.

"Routinely" means in everyday ongoing interactions. It may include such activities as analysis that has used point-of-sales (POS) data or interviews at the time of usage.

"Continuously" means that those are the most important activities of the management during the lifespan of the company.

Yet, it is not only about direct contacts with consumers and customers. There are also occasions when corollary or supplemental data can be better collected from people who have good intuition, insight, and directly related experience, in other words, people who are similar in their reaction to customers. For example, when a hospitalized patient is the consumer or "customer," it would be more appropriate to interview the nurse in charge. If a child is the consumer and customer, asking the parent is better.

Regarding the workplace, there are no conflicts between coworkers. Since all employees are people who share the same feelings about the ideological assertions of the company, conflicts are ruled out by definition. Further, there is no relative evaluation by comparison with others, since the individuality and duties of each employee are precisely determined and focus is placed on respecting individual independence. Competition is directed at improving ones own skills and achieving the "perfection of fulfilling one's own role."

Between "virtual and real" there is no conflict. Depending on the subject, it is sometimes the case that one of the two is selected as the more effective approach. Both exist in principle, however, thereby creating a unique sphere. This has become the most indispensable factor in offering unique, high-level goods and services that other firms cannot offer.

There is no conflict between the spheres "within" and "outside" the company. Indeed, the fusion between "within" and "outside" is so strong that it is difficult to distinguish between them. Until now, commodities produced inside a company have been sold outside of it. However, the distinction between "in" and "out" is a thin line that has been seen as a high wall that would require much energy to surmount. From now on, the definition of company employees will become more diverse and many types of employment relationships will serve to redefine the meaning of "inside the company." Thus, one can even say that sales to employees are already sales "outside the company."

The formation and nurturing of a customer's organization will become increasingly important. Those customers closest to the firm are already actively participating in the company just like an employee, for instance, in product development. Gradually the line dividing "in" and "out" of the company becomes thinner here as well. In the case of a really good product, customers would recommend it to other people around them and thus become part-time salespeople.

Another point, "Humbling." This suggests a modest posture. More than that, an attitude of "forceful autocracy, arrogance, and haughtiness" should by all means be avoided. The reason is that such an attitude creates a negative, even repulsive reaction in the other. Since this already constitutes conflict, it will certainly hinder the smooth progress of business.

Modesty, however, does not mean the absence of ideological assertions that can be criticized. On the contrary, preference for someone who argues his or her position well will also be there as especially then, a sympathetic response may be born.

One more point: "No competition." When products and services possess originality, a high level of professionalism, and abound in individuality, the enterprise that delivers them becomes unique — Only One — on a global scale.

If one wants to buy that product, then one can only buy from this company. Therefore, orders will arrive from all over the world. Since marketing will be unnecessary, there will be no marketing costs incurred. Similarly, due to the lack of competition, there will be no competition costs. Therefore, the money saved can be invested in enhancing the unique, Only One attributes of both the product and the company.

Let's try to put this in order.

The producer possesses a unique message — an ideological assertion. The product derives from this. Brought together by their common feeling of appreciation for this ideological assertion, people gather and form a company. Sympathizers become shareholders, suppliers, partners, and eventually customers. As a reflection of their sympathy, these people will quite naturally assert the outstanding qualities of the product to the people around them and close to them.

The assertion is met with a sympathetic response. The products flow, the concentric circles of people with sympathetic response grow. Before long the boundaries of the company, of the region, and of the country are passed and the products spread all over the world. The company has grown to a global Only One enterprise.

Given the extent of the Internet's web, it becomes possible to expand the circle of people with sympathetic response in split seconds. Three million is not a significant figure for the Internet, which is used by over 100 million people. If for instance, these 3 million people spent 3000 yen a month, it would make a sales volume of 9 billion yen per month. Accordingly, the annual sales volume would reach 100 billion yen a year.

2. The Principle of Prosperity

The main attributes of prosperity are value, continuation, spontaneity, and dissemination. It means to produce and offer what has value for the customer. It is not sufficient to offer this value just on one occasion; it must be continuously available. Quite spontaneously, this value is incorporated into the daily activities of the people around the world, and into their lifestyles. This value must then be disseminated on a global basis.

Creation of Value

The core of the matter is expressed in a Chinese saying that states that all things in this world are one and they are born from the Tao. As a result of what the Tao has produced and Virtue has nurtured, all things show this form: Vigor becomes the soul of something or, in other words, its special qualities are divinely inspired and complete.

Alternatively, we can say that "the Tao gives birth to one, one gives birth to two, two gives birth to three, and three gives birth to all things." The main points here are: "first gives birth to second and second gives birth to third."

The first, namely the Tao, gives birth to the second, namely shadow and light. Although they are two extremely different things, two gives birth to three, and three — that is the moment when the spirit rises to the sky and the feeling of "bubbling over" is born. This spirit that is rising to the sky brings about all things.

To break through and rise above heterogeneity and especially ambiguous contradictions gives birth to ideas, images, feelings, experiences, and things. Light and shadow are originally one and the same. Go back to the origin. In other words, return to the Tao. Simply, it is wonderful to balance two opposites, because then one attains the Tao. Thus the energy, the spirit to put something good out into the world, is completed. This is the secret of success in the management of value production.

Permanence

To constitute the business of a company, the creation of a product or service that has value must occur on a permanent basis. The two main characteristics of permanence are to "get rid of unnecessary extras" and "unfit for use." Do not use the energy available for unreasonable and/or redundant activities.

Additionally, always "empty everything" so the energy flow will be unrestricted. Endeavor to forget anxieties and worries. Nor should one hold on to personal possessions. Normally energy is naturally replenished, so that it can be used when it is needed.

Spontaneity

The main point is to blend into the life and lifestyles of people all over the world spontaneously and naturally. When boldness turns into courage, next is murder. When someone is frustrated and then invigorated with boldness, next one may kill himself, herself, or other people. When the absence of boldness turns into courage, next is life. A person who is invigorated without aggression can do his or her best for other people or for himself or herself. It is spontaneity, when people take and implement this themselves. However, when this is forced upon people, it is not spontaneous.

How do people take and implement this by themselves? Being dispossessed, i.e., non-attached in attitude and actuality, enables people to step into formerly impenetrable areas. What has no fixed form itself can enter into impenetrable spaces.

What has no structure can enter more easily. The way to make practical use of this is not to fix rules or determine things in advance, but rather to entrust things to the one who will use them. Rather than attempt to determine everything by oneself, it is better to do so in cooperation with the user.

Dissemination

This factor depends on and employs the "principle of development."

3. The Principle of Satisfaction

The main point of satisfaction is "knowing sufficiency." To know sufficiency is "joy and gratitude." If one thinks that something is insufficient, then it is impossible to be satisfied even when wealth is accumulated or blessings are received. In other words, satisfaction is to be found in the way one looks at something, as it is purely subjective. Thus, those who are joyful and grateful in every situation will always receive satisfaction.

Even when you achieve something, do not hang on to it. Make use of it, but do not demand it. Even if you achieve growth, do not try to dominate or restrain it.

Why? Satisfaction is achieved from the process. When you go somewhere, satisfaction does not come from arriving, but from walking there. Satisfaction arises through the production and realization processes. Once something has been produced, satisfaction is gone. Thus, the satisfaction of human beings is to be found in this "land of freedom" that one enters when one is deeply immersed in whatever it may be, when nothing else can distract or take hold of one, and when one forgets oneself.

4. The Company and the Individual

The time has come when companies and individuals (employees) have become equal. Thus, according to the three principles, "the company" and "the individual" should understand each other deeply and have mutual sympathy.

5. Human Collectivism

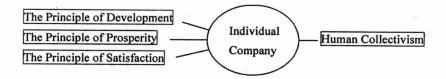

The main point here is "polish one's self," and an enterprise thus should be regarded as an appropriate "place to polish one's self." What needs to be polished? One needs to be polished into being a "Professional" and a "Leader."

What differentiates managerial leaders can be put succinctly: "people who follow the Tao." After ten to twenty years of following the Tao, they form the top layer of the company.

People of high morals, vast knowledge, and rich experience will implement the Tao when they hear it. The character of such people is as careful as someone who crosses a river in winter, or as someone who is highly alert in unfamiliar surroundings. The leader is as cold as ice — and yet as warm as the spring sun. Such leaders naturally receive admiration and respect from all sides. Since the destiny of the company depends largely on the top executives, leadership education over many years is especially crucial.

Professionalism and excellence are extremely important attributes to foster. Just as the challenges faced by celebrities in arts and sports in their respective spheres serve to stimulate their ongoing growth and development, they also need to be present in order for company employees, as well as management, to experience the fullness of life.

Small, rare things in one context may actually be quite large and numerous in another. Things will become easy, if one takes care when there is no danger, and when one deals with things as soon as there are early signs that action is necessary.

Polish your intuition to foresee and foretell things and soon you will be able to recognize some form or some thing. Even though nothing exciting seems to be visible, it will soon become so.

We must also examine organizational excellence. In the next section we discuss how to build up a business team that surpasses the organizational strength and mobility of even first class orchestras or soccer teams.

6. Strategic Organization

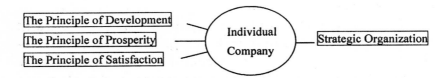

"Flexibility" is the main point here. Soft at birth, the human body stiffens in death. In other words, the condition of being firm and inflexible is already an attribute of death, whereas the attributes of life are softness and lightness. Hence, softness is the most superior physical state in the world.

The softest substance in the world — water — manipulates and governs the hardest rock. Being non-attached enables people to step into otherwise impenetrable areas. Since water is soft and formless it can enter any tiny crack. Water is what the perfect substance ought to be. While giving a harvest to all, water uses all things, and without competition it lives in symbiosis with the world. As a result, it continues to the satisfaction of everyone.

When considering the corporate organization as a strategic team, the most important aspect is achieving the goal. What underlying strategy will allow the organization to fully achieve its goal? The answer is "weakness surpasses firmness." For instance, whether the goal is to develop a new, epoch-making product or to establish an excellent new market, it is important to have the flexibility to change the organization accordingly.

One should imagine that the goal has already been fulfilled. Then one will be able to recognize the most suitable members and determine the best organizational structure in order to achieve it. If deemed necessary, this might mean hiring those with the requisite knowledge, skills, and experience from outside the firm. According to the motto "turning outside sources into internal sources," one should consider all human resources in the world as internal resources of the company.

Ranging from flexibility in organizational concepts and definitions of employment to that which is necessary to reconstitute the organizational structure as needed in order to move with change, I believe the creation and nurturance of a "creative and flexible organization" will be the essential key for the future corporate strategic organization.

Epilogue

THE HUMAN RACE IS NOW AT A TURNING POINT. Society will either be improved, or it will worsen. Clearly, we must improve it. So, what should we do?

I believe that radical change is necessary.

Although the application of Western rationalism has certainly benefited humanity materially, a heavy price has been paid for following its ways.

Reflecting upon Japan's history, there has never been a period of time like the present when Western ideals were so dominant. Thus, it is natural for us to attend now to the basics of Eastern thinking. Perhaps only when the two complements of Western and Eastern thinking have balanced will one be able to begin to find the basic underlying truth.

A creative synthesis of Western and Eastern thinking has been far too neglected.

Is this not a great loss, especially in the area of the company and its management?

In order to stir a lively debate, I would like to discuss these topics with both the broad public as well as those more directly and professionally concerned. I believe that the pursuit of truth will be served by furthering discussion on a global scale.

Pragmatically, the Internet is the most suitable tool for realizing this goal. Currently, a debate and discussion is unfolding on the Internet in the "Tao Management Forum" on the web site http://www.haruaki.co.jp/tao-management/. You are most welcome to join, and please feel free to express your opinions. We anticipate rich, earnest, and fruitful discussions.

We would like to concentrate the wisdom about Tao Management as well as nurture its steady development and utilization. In this way we may serve as a resource and perhaps even as a guide for the twenty-first- century business world, and beyond.

This is precisely what Tao Management is all about.

References

Abe, Yoshio and Toshio Yamamoto. *Ro-shi* (*Laozi*). Tokyo: Meijishoin, 1966.

Chang, Chunyuan. *Ro-shi no Shiso* (The philosophy of Lao-zi). Tokyo: Kodansha, 1987.

Fukunaga, Mitsuji. *Ro-shi* (*Laozi*). Tokyo: Asahi Shimbunsha, 1997.

Kanaya, Osamu. *Ro-shi* (*Laozi*). Tokyo: Kodansha, 1997.

Taguchi, Yoshifumi. *Bujinesu Senshi no Tameno Kofukuron* (Discourses on happiness: For Japanese business warriors). Tokyo: Takei Shuppan (now, Chichi Shuppansha), 1989.

Taguchi, Yoshifumi, *Jinsei Soncho naki Kigyo wa Horobiru* (Doomed are companies that neglect the importance of people). Tokyo: TBS Britannica, 1992.

Taguchi, Yoshifumi. *Kigyo no "Seizon Ryoiki" wo Dou Mitsukeruka* (In search of a company's survival space). Tokyo: Manejimentosha, 1992.

Taguchi, Yoshifumi. *Dai-Tenkanki: Keiei no Honshitsu* (Amidst a grand transformation: The essentials of management). Tokyo: Chichi Shuppansha, 1995.

Taguchi, Yoshifumi. *Fuhen to Sentan: Keiei no Dori* (Universality and forefront: Truth in management). Tokyo: Sanchoh Shuppansha, 1996.

EastBridge

TAO MANAGEMENT
Japanese Management Philosophy Based on
an Interpretation of the *Tao Te Ching*

Yoshifumi Taguchi

Yoshifumi Taguchi was born in Tokyo in 1942. After a successful career in the motion picture industry in the 1960s, Mr. Taguchi established a consulting company, Image Plan, where he continues to serve as CEO. Among other things, he lectures to many corporate executives in Japan and other parts of Asia. The ideas articulated in *Tao Management* are at the core of his management philosophy.